# Getting To Heaven On A Harley

*Awaken to the Truth of Who You Are
and Imagine Your Own 'Life Review'*

(A 'Radical Karma' Workbook)

# COLIN C. TIPPING

Award-Winning Author of *Radical Forgiveness,
Making Room for the Miracle*

**Getting to Heaven on a Harley —**
*Awaken to the Truth of Who You Are and Imagine Your Own 'Life Review'*
A 'Radical Karma' Workbook

Date of Publication: March, 2008

ISBN **978-0-978699-37-6**

Global 13 Publications, Inc.
26 Briar Gate Lane
Marietta, GA 30066
sales@radicalforgiveness.com


Web Site: **www.radicalforgiveness.com**

Cover Design: Colin Tipping
Cover Art: Artist Unknown
Illustrations: JoAnn Tipping
Line Editing: Shari Claire
Proof Reading: Keith Ely

This book is dedicated to the members of my men's group,
collectively known as the Chiron Brotherhood:

**Farra Allen, Dennis McCauley, George Poirier,
Gregory Possman, Joe Teagarden and Jack Winner**

without whose love and support over the
period from 1996 to present day,
I might never have found
my power and
my voice.

# ACKNOWLEDGMENTS

There are so many people I need to thank for having a direct or indirect hand in helping me come to the point in my life where I was able to write this book, but none more deserving of my gratitude and love than my wife, JoAnn. As my partner in presenting our Radical Forgiveness and Radical Manifestation workshops to groups all around the world, she has helped me to formulate and refine the concepts and ideas of both, and as such, is jointly responsible for the how this book evolved out of our working together.

I also stand on the shoulders of many wonderful authors and speakers, sages and wits whose works and words have inspired and excited me over the years, but none more so than Arnold Patent, the author of *You Can Have it All* and other books. Back in the late 80s, I was listening to a tape by Arnold that someone had given me and I heard him say in answer to a question, ***"Listen, forgiveness is not letting bygones be bygones. It's recognizing that nothing wrong ever happened."*** Those words electrified me, and the rest is history as they say.

But that history is replete with many other beautiful and wonderful people who have helped me, encouraged me and lifted me up in so many ways. I am very grateful for them being in my life.

My thanks, too, for my business partners, coaches, co-workers, trainers and facilitators who do such a great job of supporting the work, both here in the U.S. and in other countries around the world — Hina and Thomas Fruh in Germany, Ireneusz Rudnicki and Irena Rutenberg in Poland, Sailaja Jonnalagadda in India and Chris Hooper in Australia. Special thanks go to our director of training, Karla Garrett, for overseeing the training of all our coaches in the U.S., David Klosen for the distribution of product, and Shari Claire who, besides being the company 'techie' and webmaster, as director of operations takes the pressure off me in all sorts of ways so I can be free to write and be creative. I am so blessed to have such wonderful people to help me.

If you like this book and find it helpful, please keep in mind how much you owe these people and many more besides, because without them I doubt it ever would have been written.

# The Author

Born in England in 1941, Colin was raised during the war and in early post-war Britain by working-class parents. By his own account, his parents were good people, loving and hard working, and he considers himself blessed by having had a stable and enjoyable childhood in spite of the social hardships of the time.

Even as a boy, he seemed to inspire the trust of people who needed to talk about their feelings, they finding in him a person who would listen to them and not judge. After a four year stint in the Royal Air Force, he became a High School teacher and a college professor, but even then often found himself being sought after to provide counseling for people. He has three children from his first marriage which ended in divorce after seven years. A second marriage lasted only four, but he nevertheless remains friends with both ex-wives. He has 10 grandchildren from his first marriage.

He emigrated in 1984 to America and shortly thereafter became certified as a clinical hypnotherapist. He liked hypnotherapy because, he concluded after some years of experience, it speeded up the therapy at least by a factor of three.

He was not religious then and still feels free of any organized religious dogma. His spirituality is essentially practical and down-to-earth, simple, free and open-ended. While he never claims to know the truth and is happy to live in the mystery of the question, he loves to muse and create *stories* that at least make sense to our limited minds and resonate with our inner knowingness. He has a knack of making spiritual issues simple and practical. He believes that spirituality is useless if it cannot be used in a practical way in our everyday life. His books all have a practical side to them as do his workshops.

In 1992, he and his wife JoAnn, whom he met in Atlanta and married in 1990, created a series of healing retreats in the North Georgia mountains for people challenged by cancer. In recognizing that lack of forgiveness was a big part of the causation, they set about refining a new form of forgiveness that had to be quick, easy to do, simple and therapy free. This was later to become what is now recognized as Radical Forgiveness. He now has an Institute for Radical Forgiveness in the U.S.A., Australia, India, Poland and Germany.

Since writing his first award winning book, *Radical Forgiveness, Making Room for the Miracle* in 1998, Colin and JoAnn have together facilitated regular workshops stateside and overseas, while keeping a base in Atlanta, Georgia, where they offer their renowned *Miracles* workshop at the retreat center in the North Georgia mountains. He is also now offering workshops based on his new book, *Radical Manifestation, the Fine Art of Creating the Life You Want.*

He has recently launched a major initiative to take a specialized form of the Radical Forgiveness technology into corporations and other organizations, as a way of resolving and preventing conflict, raising morale and increasing productivity. It is called The Quantum Energy Management System. Colin's recent book, *Spiritual Intelligence At Work,* explains the rationale for this system.

His mission statement is as follows: ***"My Mission is to raise the consciousness of the planet through Radical Forgiveness and create a world of forgiveness by 2012."***

He has no plans to retire any time soon!

More information at **www.radicalforgiveness.com**

# Contents

# INTRODUCTION

There are some fundamental questions that have taxed the minds of both philosophers and ordinary people ever since we developed the capacity to think abstractly. The main ones are:

Who are we?
What are we?
Why are we here?
What is the meaning of our lives?
What is the meaning of our death?

It is understandable that we have tended to focus our attention on proposing answers to the last of these, since it is the only one that has an urgent and practical relevance to every human being on the planet capable of rational thought. We are all marching inexorably towards death and who among us is not concerned about what happens when we get there?

There are literally thousands of myths that endeavor to explain the nature of death, but fundamentally they come down to two diametrically opposing ideas. The first one is clear, simple and straightforward — nothing happens. The argument is that death for us is no different from the death of a tree in that, just as the life-force of a tree ceases to flow when it is felled, so the life force of a human being collapses the moment the heart stops beating, or at least very soon afterwards. This myth states that upon death, life simply ceases and the body decomposes. End of story.

The second idea, which is central to thousands of variations on the same general theme, is that the body dies but the soul, or the spiritual essence of the person, which existed even before it took on a body, carries on in some form of afterlife. The variations on this theme are many and varied,

1

with the notion of our going to either Heaven or Hell, depending on our worthiness, being the most simplistic and therefore probably the most widely accepted myth. At the other end of the scale we find the most sophisticated and mystical notions about the nature of death in *The Tibetan Book of the Living and Dying*.

The fact is, of course, that nobody really knows. All of our notions about death and the afterlife are just myths. Some are just plain silly, but others carry an enormous degree of intellectual, emotional and spiritual weight with the vast majority of the world population, including those with the strongest intellects and most developed wisdom. Great philosophers throughout the ages have found myths that propose an afterlife for the soul worthy of acceptance and, of course, most worldwide religions are founded on the basic myth that the soul is eternal.

At a more prosaic level, I find the most intriguing 'evidence' for life after death coming from the great wealth of admittedly circumstantial, subjective and anecdotal evidence (the kind much hated and derided by scientists, I hasten to add), found in the copious literature from all around the world on the phenomenon of the near death experience (NDE).

As the name implies, a near death experience is where a person experiences what seems to be a clinical death but actually recovers, and then goes on to recount what happened on the *other side* while they were *dead.* The striking thing about all these accounts from all over the world by just ordinary everyday people, is their marked similarity.

They all describe much the same thing — being drawn up into a tunnel of beautiful white light while moving towards some kind of loving *presence,* often with previously departed loved-ones there to welcome them. The most universal aspect to everyone's story is their report of the intense love that emanated from the presence and how loved and accepted they felt, like nothing they had ever experienced on Earth. They almost all report being told that they were not finished yet and needed to go back. Most of them really didn't want to. The overwhelming love they felt in the realm they'd apparently entered into was so blissful they didn't want to leave, but they had no choice.

Some of them got a little further along and reported going through a life review process. They reported being shown a *movie* of their lives so they could see the consequences of every decision they had ever made. But they were never subjected to judgment about it. There has never been one single report of punishment or mention of Hell.

They all seem to undergo a profound change in how they subsequently saw their own lives in contrast to how they had seen them before. It was as if they had seen beyond the veil and now understood the meaning of it all. They no longer worried because they now had a profound trust of life that came from knowing that they were being taken care of no matter what the outer circumstances. They had an inner peace.

Some scientists have done their best to give rational, brain-centered explanations of NDEs but those that I have been exposed to seem to me to stretch credulity far more thinly than the very idea they are trying to refute. Science is not well suited to explaining spiritual phenomena.

Now, as far as I know, there have been no confirmed reports of anyone making the journey into the tunnel on a Harley Davidson motorcycle, but anything is possible as you are about to find out when you read the story coming up ahead.

In the story which forms Part One of this book my lead character, Steve Parker, dies in a motorcycle accident and eventually, after having some adventures in the *in-between* phase with another *dead* guy he befriends, finds himself speeding up the tunnel of light on a Harley Davidson. The irony of this is not that he has been fixated all his life on this make of motorcycle and actually died by crashing one, but that his Angel of Incarnation who would take him through his life review was named Harley. (Harley is also featured in another of my books — *A Radical Incarnation.*) When he was in a body, Harley loved those bikes too.

3

Harley takes Steve through his life review and Steve gets to meet his soul group. These are the souls he made pre-incarnation agreements with and with whom he interacted in his own lifetime in service to those agreements, each carrying out their side of the bargain. Others were souls who had supported him throughout his life from the other side.

The purpose of the story is to support the very myth that is the heart and soul of my concept of Radical Forgiveness. This is explained here in this book only as much as it is necessary to support the reader, but the basic reference for it, for those who want a more in-depth explanation, is my first book *Radical Forgiveness, Making Room for the Miracle.* The basic assumptions of Radical Forgiveness you will find in the Preface to Part Four on Page 159 of this book.

Parts Two and Three are about YOU. They ask you first to imagine what your Radical Life Review would be like if you went through it now, taking it not from the normal perspective of you having made mistakes, done some bad things, had bad things happen to you, etc., but from the Radical Forgiveness point of view that it was all perfect and Divinely guided. Second, you get the opportunity to use this model to map out how you want to create your life from this point on. Part Four provides specific information about the Radical Forgiveness tools.

My hope is that this book will help you to answer for yourself those questions: Who am I? What am I? Why am I here? What is the meaning of my life? And, what will I do next? I also trust that you will enjoy the experience of coming to see your life as Divinely guided and totally perfect in every way.

Colin Tipping                                                    March 2008

# PART ONE

# Steve Parker's Story

*To Heaven on A Harley*

# Chapter 1
## Beginning at the End

Finally, I died. What was most surprising, though, given the circumstances, was that death actually came quite easy. Not knowing what to expect, the final few minutes leading up to it had been painful and frightening even though I was only half conscious. Everyone around me had been frantic and desperate to save my life, but to no avail. It had been a terrible accident.

There I stood, injury free, completely detached; just observing; peaceful. My body lay crumpled and distorted with both legs arranged at very odd angles relative to my torso, broken in several places. My head, with my mop of grey hair soaked in blood, was twisted at an unnatural angle and there was blood everywhere. Not a pretty sight. The mangled condition of my motorcycle hinted at how fast I might have been going when I lost control, skidded and collided with the tree. Probably around 95 miles an hour.

As usual, I had been venting my anger by driving fast. It was one of the many ways I dealt with my rage and the pain that lay beneath it. Riding that bike with the wind in my face gave me a sense of freedom; it was my escape. Clearly, though, this time I had paid the price.

An ambulance drew up with lights ablaze. "No use, pal." said the police officer who had come upon the scene almost immediately, along with some people who had stopped to help, "He's a goner."

The medics took one look and the senior one of the two concurred simply with a nod. "Must have been goin' like a bat out of Hell," he said looking first at my mangled body and then at the even more mangled motorcycle. "This has always been a treacherous corner. We've scraped up quite a few at this spot over the years, but they don't do anything about making it any safer."

"I'll put it in a report," replied the police officer sardonically as he watched the medics begin the gruesome task of lifting my bloody and twisted corpse onto the stretcher. "I have his wallet, so at least we know who he is. One of our boys will have to break the news, I suppose, to whomever he was either leaving or going home to. I hate that job, so I hope it doesn't fall to me."

"Now come on you folks. Nothing more to be done here now," he said addressing all those kind people who had stopped and tried to save me. "Let's move on now — and wherever you're headed, do drive carefully."

"He was no spring chicken," said the younger medic when the public had dispersed. "Bit old for a biker, I'd say, especially the kind of speed he must have been going on that bike. Powerful one too."

The police officer checked the date on my driving license. "A few months over 65," he said. "Would have qualified for Medicare if he'd made it. Shame, isn't it? Work all those years just to get to retirement age and then poof! Gone. Makes you think, don't it?"

"Mmm," murmured both medics, clearly preferring not to think about it. They had a job to do and as far as they were concerned, it didn't make it any less unpleasant to think a whole lot about it. "I guess you'll have a wrecker pick up the bike?" asked the senior of the two, anxious to get back to the business at hand.

At that moment, I had a really strong urge to make myself apparent to them. I was even wondering if I was really dead, or whether I was just having an out-of-body experience, or dreaming. "Hey, that's my body you've got there," I shouted to the medics as they loaded me into the ambulance. I felt panic at the thought of being separated from my body. "Take me with you," I pleaded. Zero response. The ambulance and police car drove off just as the wrecker came and picked up the wreck that had been my pride and joy. I felt very alone and abandoned.

Traffic soon resumed its normal whoosh, whoosh sound as cars and trucks sped by, drivers and passengers blissfully unaware that my death had just occurred only moments ago, right at this spot. They were also totally unaware of my ethereal presence standing by the side of the road where my body had been. All that was left now as evidence of what had occurred was the dark blood stain, but even that was being washed away by the rain that had begun to drizzle steadily.

As the traffic continued to rush by totally oblivious of my presence I felt an overwhelming and crushing sense of separation and aloneness. I was disconnected from my human existence and yet I yearned desperately to be reunited with my body again. I wanted to go back and talk to my wife and kids and tell them how sorry I was for being such an asshole, and then to make it right. The compassion I felt for them at that moment engulfed me.

I was particularly concerned about Verna, my current wife. Tall, slender and brown-eyed with long dark hair that she wore in a pony tail most of the time; she was quite lovely. We had been married for 10 years but it was not an easy relationship. In spite of the fact that we shared the same kind of spiritual beliefs and did our best to live up to them in our relationship, there was always tension. My anger was quick to flare and she would go into defense every time. Her previous husband was physically abusive so she always reacted this way whenever I got activated. It was all the worse for her knowing that the cause of my anger was rooted in the death of the woman I had been married to before her.

Nevertheless, the love was there beneath it all and I knew that my death would be hitting her hard. She depended on me a great deal and would be feeling very lost and alone. I desperately needed to tell her how much I loved her and how sorry I was that I so often took out my anger on her. Right before I took that fateful ride on my Harley Davidson, I had stormed out of the house in anger and left without saying a thing to her. If only I could go back and tell her that I loved her and that it wasn't about her. It was about Susan.

Susan was my second wife and, really and truly, the love of my life. To look at, she was the opposite of Verna. She was petite and wore her fair hair very short. She had the most amazing green eyes that sparkled and shone all the time. She was a dancer. We were inseparable and were a couple for life. That much we both knew. I was 35 when I married her. She was 27. Seven years later she was dead at 34. I was absolutely devastated. I went down fast. Alcohol, drugs, gratuitous sex and getting involved in get rich schemes one after the other, were the markers for my life during the next six years. I was a terrible mess and was heading for oblivion.

But it was during that time that I began to search for some meaning in my life. I had to find something that I could latch onto that might alleviate the pain of losing Susan and give some explanation of her death. Without that, I knew I would self-destruct. I was already close to doing so. One day, a friend of mine sent me a book called *Radical Forgiveness.* I put it aside for more than a year — didn't even open it. I never mentioned it to my friend and he never asked me about it. Then one day, after a terrible night of drinking, I picked it up and began reading it. I couldn't put it down. That book put everything about my life into perspective for me and my healing began. It basically saved my life.

My kids were from my first marriage. I married June when I was in the Navy. I was only 22 and totally irresponsible. I messed around with other women — one in every port as they say — so the marriage was flawed from the start. We soon produced a couple of kids in quick succession, one boy and one girl. By that time I was out of the Navy, but I was unsettled and couldn't hold a job down for more than a few months at a time. Our third baby died — a crib death. SIDS they call it. Sudden Infant Death Syndrome.

They give it a name but don't understand the cause of it and that makes it worse. June blamed herself and she never really got over it. She became very depressed and remote and I just didn't know how to cope with her.

So things got very unpleasant and after 10 years of marriage, we divorced. Of course the children were devastated and they have never really forgiven me. I disappeared out of their lives almost totally and didn't try to reconnect until after I had read the *Radical Forgiveness* book and started my journey towards healing and wholeness. Neither one of them would have anything to do with me, and I can't say I blame them.

But, I wondered what they would say when they learned that I had died? Would they wish they could have forgiven me even if it were just a little bit? Would they begin to wonder who their father really was, now that I was gone? I wished I could go back and connect with them now. Might they feel the same way?

Even while I was feeling this powerful urge to go back and clean up the mess of my life, I began to notice a strong pull in the opposite direction. I didn't connect with it at the time, but was later to discover that it was an invitation to begin moving towards the light. But I wasn't ready for that yet.

"Hey!"

The owner of this voice appeared out of nowhere. Disheveled and covered in dirt and what looked like dried blood, he was still dressed in a suit, white shirt and tie. The tie hung loose but was still more or less in place. He was medium height and, in spite of advancing years, was still relatively slim. He looked like he had worked out a lot and taken care of his looks.

11

Although filthy dirty, underneath the grime he was probably an attractive looking guy. He was somewhere around 60 years old. Not much younger than me.

"You too, eh?" he said. "Well, you're not the first to buy it on this bend. Neither am I. Lots of people have died here. Actually, I saw you coming on that bike of yours and knew it was going to happen. It was inevitable. Watched the whole thing. Very dramatic. Were you drunk?"

"No," I snapped back quickly.

"Stoned then?"

"No. I wasn't stoned either. Just angry as Hell."

"Same thing," he countered. "Anger is just another addiction. Any addiction will get you in the end. I was drunk as a skunk when I hit that bend in my brand new Jag. Died instantly but it was a while before I realized it. I kept talking to everyone but they didn't hear or see me which really made me mad. I thought they were ignoring me because I was drunk. Finally I got it that I was dead. What a shock that was!"

"How long ago was that?"

"I don't know. Can't tell. It seems like forever, but for me time has stopped, so I have no idea. My watch still registers the time of my death."

I looked at my own watch and noticed it too was stopped at the time of my own death. I guess time is nonexistent on this side. I looked at this guy and felt a great sadness come over me. He seemed stuck or trapped somehow. I became immediately concerned that I might be in the same predicament. I could still feel the mysterious pull towards something that would take me someplace else beyond my understanding, but the thought occurred to me that I might be trapped too.

"Why are you still here?" I asked, nervously.

"Because of that, I think." He pointed to a white painted cross planted in the earth. It was adorned with plastic flowers, shells, photos and other memorabilia. The name Joseph was painted on the horizontal bar of the crudely made cross. "It's like I'm stuck to that thing. It won't let me go. They won't let me go."

"Who's they?"

"My family. They can't get over my dying in an accident. They hang on to me. They drive by this cross virtually every day and slow down as they go by. They have to slow down anyway because of the bend, but they look over with sad faces."

"They must have loved you a lot," I offered.

"Ah! They say they loved me but they really blame me because of my drinking. My wife is like you – angry. This thing is their way of showing their grief but they don't realize how it fixes me to this Earth plane, or rather the astral plane which is where you and I are right now. Just one level above the Earth plane but not yet in the world of Spirit. A kind of never-never land. We're between the two worlds, you and I, mister. But if you are smart, you'll move quickly towards the light that they all keep talking to me about, before your family does things like this to keep you stuck."

"Maybe you're not as stuck as you think you are," I suggested. "Perhaps it's your own shame that holds you back. Frightened of being judged, are you? Of being sent to Hell because of your drinking and all the other stuff that went with it?"

Though neither one of us had an awareness of time and therefore could not tell how long he had been held by the chords of energy that held Joseph captive to his family by virtue of their having placed this memorial at the place of his death, I did notice that the wooden members of the memorial were losing their paint and were turning green with algae. This was a sure sign that it had been there for some months. The photos too were completely faded and curled. The only things that remained as colored now as on the day the memorial was placed, were the plastic flowers which, since they didn't degrade, denied the man's death just as much as they resisted decay. In doing so, they gave a perverse comfort to those who drove by each day with sad faces. Real flowers would have degraded a long time ago thereby confirming the death of Joseph P. Noland. Plastic flowers prolonged the agony and held him captive longer than it took for natural flowers to droop and die.

He sat silent for a while, thinking. He turned and took a long look at the cross, twisting his head hard round in the process. "Maybe so. I certainly had religion pumped into me when I was a kid, though I didn't follow through much as an adult. Heard a lot about God being an angry, judgmental piece of work who would throw me into Hell at the drop of a hat if he thought I had sinned. My rotten dad pumped that into me all right. Well, I sinned a good bit, I admit that. Drink was the worst but besides the drinking I committed adultery a lot. Loose women – even prostitutes now and again if pushed. Mostly married women actually. I found them the easiest to seduce with a few kind words and expensive gifts. Never hardly gave it a thought, even though I was married to a good woman. I feel bad about it now, though. I know it really hurt her. She knew, even though she didn't say much about it, at least after the third time she caught me at it. Basically gave up on me. But she stayed with me though. Can't think why, really. For the money perhaps. I did bring home the bacon and she didn't want for anything, I will say that. I never kept her short, honestly."

He sat silently for a while. I couldn't tell whether he was nostalgically going back over some of his sexual exploits or contemplating the likelihood of paying a heavy price for them if and when he made it to the 'pearly gates.'

14

"I think you're right," he said, turning his head towards me so he could look at me directly. "I am scared to death of that judgment. I feel sure I will be going to Hell. I'm thinking I'll have to do what the two other guys who were already here when I got here, decided to do. They were in the same predicament. One of them was a pedophile and the other a murderer so they were certain they had no chance of getting into Heaven."

"What did they do?" I inquired, wondering what my own options might be once I had taken stock of my chances of getting a pass. I wasn't feeling all that optimistic about that. I hadn't been as much of a schmuck as this Joseph guy, or the two he spoke about, but I'd been no angel either. I'd done a lot of dumb things in my life and hurt a lot of people. I married a woman I shouldn't, had two kids with her and left after ten years. I virtually abandoned my kids. They didn't really know me and wouldn't give me time of day now. I didn't blame them either. I was so caught up with my own life, I really didn't give them much thought, so why should they bother with me now that I was old? I wondered what they would think now that I was gone. Good riddance probably. My second wife, the love of my life, died of cancer. Not wanting to be alone, I married Verna, my current wife of ten years, but I treated her badly. I was too angry about losing Susan and I took it out on Verna. I had so much anger. Just as I was beginning to get over it, finding love for Verna, and creating a job I loved, I had to go and get killed. Damn!

"They decided that going towards the light was too risky, so they made a decision to stay around on the Earth plane by attaching themselves to a living person and thereby live vicariously through them. Apparently it is really easy to slip inside a living person, but it is especially easy if the person is drunk, on drugs, or under anesthetic. So the best place to go to find likely candidates is either a bar or a hospital. Consequently, they headed off to one or the other. Actually being a drunkard, I'd have been a perfect candidate, especially for a discarnate spirit who had been a drinker. He or she could easily have got their fix through me. I certainly drank as if I were drinking for a whole bunch of people. Maybe that's why I was able to hold my drink so well. For all I know, I might have had a whole bunch of them in my energy field helping me suck up the alcohol. If I did, I have no idea what might have happened to them when I croaked. Dashed off to find another host, I guess."

I could certainly understand the logic of this, but as I briefly considered it as an option for myself, it didn't seem right. I didn't really buy into the idea of God being an angry, judgmental and punishing entity that would wish eternal fire and damnation to be visited upon me for having made some bad judgment calls during my lifetime. Neither did I believe in Hell except the one we created for ourselves on Earth. I had always thought of God as a loving and forgiving old guy with nary a judgment in his mind. Even though I had been a real jerk during my life, I felt very sure he would accept me unconditionally when I showed up at the gates of Heaven.

So, in that moment I decided against that strategy. I really didn't want to hang around the Earth plane living in someone else's body, though I have to admit that I was still yearning to get back into my own body to continue my human journey. I didn't want it to be over. There was so much more that I wanted to do. As I mentioned previously, I had just found a purpose for my life in the work that I had recently taken up. It was giving me personal satisfaction as well as helping other people. I wanted to do more of it.

"Let me make a suggestion," I said to this guy who was now looking so forlorn, scared and dejected. "I think you are wrong about this. I think God will forgive you. He understands that you have an addictive personality. You played it out through sex and drink and that's all there is to it. He'll understand. Look, as much as I want to go back, I don't fancy the idea of parking my energy in someone else's body. It's either my own or none at all. So I'm going to respond to this pull I am feeling to move towards the light. Why don't you come with me? Maybe I can ask for dispensation on your behalf if they give you a hard time at the gate. What do you think?"

"What about this?" he said, pointing to the memorial planted by the roadside by his loved ones. "Don't I have a duty to stay by this? Won't my family feel I have let them down? Surely they will know that I have left."

"Even if they do, that's their problem. They have to deal with their own grief and anger about your life and your death. You hanging out here won't help them. Anyway, it's only your own guilt that keeps you trapped. So, just leave it and come with me."

He was clearly struggling with this. Fear gripped him. He sat there looking at the cross with all the plastic decorations on it, obviously feeling the pull of his family and the symbolism that the memorial suggested, some of it light and some dark. Finally, he jerked his head around to look at me again. "All right," he said. "Let's do it." But then he thought for a moment and said, "But not until we've had one more drink here on Earth."

"What are you talking about?" I demanded to know. Joe seemed to have come alive, hopefully at the prospect of moving towards the light but more likely at the thought of a drink. "How can we have a drink? First of all this body isn't real anymore and no one can see us anyway, so unless we find some psychic clairvoyant barman who would be perfectly comfortable serving spirits to a couple of spirits, we're screwed."

"No, that's not how we'd do it," said Joe. "We simply go to a bar, find a couple of guys who are already quite inebriated and leap in for a while. Have them order up a couple of stiff drinks and we're away. They won't know the difference. We stay for a while and then leave. Then we'll go to the light."

"You can't go to the light drunk," I protested. "God will smell it on your breath!"

"What breath?" countered Joe. "You're dead and without a body, so how can you have breath?"

17

"Oh, yes. I forgot. But it's one thing to die drunk like you did, but quite another to get drunk on the way to Heaven, don't you think? They're bound to know. I bet they'll take a dim view of that even if they are inclined to forgive sins committed on Earth."

"Oh, come on. Just one drink and then we'll go to the light together. By the way, I'm Joe Noland, what's your name?

"Steve Parker. But the answer is still no," I replied, extending my hand out to shake his bloody stained hand.

"OK, Steve, tell you what. We do the one drink and then together we'll pay a quick visit to your wife and we'll give her a sign that you are OK and that she isn't to worry anymore. I'm too far gone to be able to make anything happen on the Earth plane, but you are still fresh enough to be able to manifest something of a physical nature that she would recognize as a sign from you. What do you think? Is it a deal? For the first time since I died, I feel free – from obligation to my family, free from guilt and free from all my old addictions. You have helped me so much. So let's celebrate this the old way, just once more."

I thought about it for a moment. "Well, even though I don't have a body anymore, it sure feels as though I could use a drink. A brandy would be wonderful. And I do want to pay one last visit to Verna. She will be in a lot of pain but it would make a big difference if she knew that I was contacting her and letting her know that I love her. I didn't tell her that often enough. But I'm not staying a moment longer in any dude's body than it takes to feel the effect of one drink, OK? One drink and that's it."

# Chapter 2
# A Place to Park

The barmaid served them each another drink and marked their tabs. Brian and James were regulars at this bar and invariably met each day after work. They were journalists and liked to meet up to share stories before going home on the train. At least that was their excuse. The truth was that they were both heavy drinkers — almost certainly alcoholics. For each of them, these two or three drinks after work were the first of what would be many throughout the evening.

Brian was sharing a juicy story with James about some male politician who had been caught in a compromising situation with a male prostitute, when out of the corner of her eye, Wendy, the barmaid noticed both of them make a jerking movement. It was simultaneous but neither of them seemed to notice. It was almost imperceptible but Wendy saw it. It was something she had seen before in other serious drinkers but never had she seen two people do it in unison. She felt a shiver go down her spine, and she didn't know why. She felt the need to move away from the two young journalists even though they were regulars and often chatted with her. Something was making her feel uncomfortable.

Brian suddenly felt the need to have a brandy. It was not normally his drink but Wendy served it anyway without a word said. James, on the other hand, queried it. "Brandy? I don't see you drinking that very often. What's come over you, all of a sudden?"

"I don't know, I just felt the need for it. A sudden urge. You're right, whiskey is normally my drink this time of day. I might have a brandy after dinner, but that's not often. Do you want one? Keep me company?"

"I don't think so, but I have a bit of a hankering for a beer at the moment, so I think I'll do that. Wendy. Give me a bottle of my usual, please."

Neither said anything about it, but both were feeling a little strange. Not drunk, for both of them could take their drink, but a little odd nevertheless. Eventually Brian came close to falling off his stool, prompting Wendy to suggest they both had had enough.

# Chapter 3
# Unwelcome Guest

Brian was my choice but I wasn't expecting the kind of reception I got. "Hey, who the Hell are you? This is my turf. Who said you could muscle in as if you own the place? I've been parked here a long time and I don't intend to move out or even share this space. This boy's a steady drinker so I get a good regular fix. I'm not having any recently expired jackass move in on me. Got it? So scram!"

"One drink and I'm gone. I promise," I replied hastily, taken aback at finding another spirit inhabiting Brian's body and thinking that probably appeasement was the best policy. "But tell me, why do you stay? Didn't you have enough of this crap while you were human? Why not go to the light? You could come with us if you want. Heaven is a great place. No addictions. No pain to medicate with booze, just love and harmony. You're welcome to join us. Won't you do it?"

"It's not for the likes of me, mate," he said. "They'd more 'an likely send me downstairs if you know what I mean. I can't take that kind of heat if you get my drift. I'm better orf, 'ere. I needs my drink, anyway and it's not so bad being parked here, except I have to keep defending my turf, just like when I was a barra boy down the East End. Always people tryin' to pinch your place. You'd be amazed at how many spooks want to park here wi' me, but I won't 'ave it, y'see. I likes my privacy so I chuck 'em all out, regular like. Some spooks do this and make a community of it, but I like to be alone. Makes it simpler for my big guy too. Too many in here and he might begin feeling weird and confused. Might begin thinking he needed to stop drinkin'. Then where'd I be? Know what I mean? OK, now take that drink and 'oppit."

The cockney accent and belligerent attitude worthy of any sales-cart vendor (a barrow-boy in England), plying his wares on the streets in the East End of London, belied the underlying fear that kept him indefinitely attached to his host. Brian, of course, had no idea that he had any kind of a spook attached to him, let alone one with a cockney accent. Neither did he realize that he kept a spook nicely supplied with alcohol. He might have been grateful though, that the spook with a cockney accent was fighting to keep other spooks out who otherwise might wish to set up a community in there.

"Are you sure you won't come along?" I asked again, having imbibed the drink somehow and was now ready to move out. "You won't go to Hell, I promise. This is Hell, down here. The light will set you free. Why don't you come?"

"Screw you, and leave me alone. 'Oppit!" he shouted, waving his arms violently.

"Your choice," I replied. "Now, how do I get out of here?" I thought. The moment I had that thought, I was out, but I must have been clumsy in doing so, for Brian acted for a second or two as if he was having a seizure. He'd had one foot just touching the ground and the other up on the chair rail taking most of his weight. As he jerked, that foot slipped off the rail which meant that he was completely off balance for a moment or two. He recovered enough not to fall over completely but meanwhile had emptied his glass all over James as he staggered and grabbed at anything nearby that would stop him from falling over completely. "I think you might have had enough for tonight," Wendy commented. Brian protested and yet couldn't fathom why he had made such an idiot of himself.

When Brian was mid-fall and spilling his drink all over James, I heard a loud shriek. I knew it had not emanated from either Brian or James. It had come from the spook with a cockney accent who upon seeing his supply of alcohol spilling over was cursing me in my clumsiness. When he heard the barmaid suggest a cessation of any further drinking, he wailed again. But at least I was out. The next question was where was Joe? Had he emerged yet?

Momentarily Joe appeared at my side, looking decidedly cool and relaxed. No less disheveled and dirty but relaxed nevertheless. "That's better," he said. "Let's go visit Verna."

"Did you find other company in James?" I asked.

"Sure did," replied Joe. "Quite a bunch of them. Not a friendly crowd either, except one female. She was quite welcoming and I felt all the old stirrings in my loins again, but I knew it was no good. Viagra without the physical means to respond to it is my version of Hell so I knew better than to try. How about you?"

"One belligerent old cockney guy from London's East End. Rough crowd down at that end, they tell me. He wasn't so bad but he wanted me gone as soon as I had soaked up some alcohol fumes. Very territorial. I tried to get him to come with me, but he wouldn't hear of it. Hell, fire and damnation and all that. You know the story."

Joe and I found our way to my house. Verna was in a state of deep sleep which was good because I didn't want to scare her by showing up as some kind of apparition in her space. I would enter her dream cycle and communicate that way. I waited for some rapid eye movement that would indicate that she was dreaming.

When the eye movement started, I whispered into her ear, telling her that I loved her and that I was OK. I asked her to help me go to the light by forgiving me, if it were possible, for being mad at her and abandoning her this way. I explained that it would make a huge difference if I could go on without having to take emotional baggage with me. Her forgiveness would

23

release me. If she held on to it, it would be a drag on me and on her too. I told her that I released her completely and that she was to carry no guilt about my death. I stroked her hair as she lay there, but I could feel nothing and was certain that she would not have sensed it either. I said all that I needed to say and felt complete. I was so pleased I came to her in this way and felt OK now about leaving her.

# Chapter 4
# The Dream

Verna awoke with a start. Instinctively she moved her arm over to feel his presence and connect with his nice warm body as she had done for years upon waking. It took her about half a second to remember the awful truth. He was dead. He'd been dead for a week and he would never lay beside her again. She quickly withdrew her arm as the pain of her realization shot through her body like an electric shock and the terrible sadness returned.

It had been a week since the police officer had knocked on her door and informed her that her Steve had been killed in an accident. She had gone weak at the knees and almost passed out upon hearing the terrible news. It was almost more than she could bear, but at the time no tears had come. That was still the case one week later. It was as if she had died too. She was in terrible pain while at the same time numbed out. Immobilized.

It was the dream that had suddenly awakened her. She was not one to dream much and when she did they seldom made any sense. They were never coherent, just a collection of unrelated images and thoughts. And she hardly ever remembered them upon waking. This one was different. It had such clarity and realism that she had to do a double take again in those few seconds after waking to convince herself that she hadn't just dreamed Steve's death. For a fraction of second there was that spark of hope but it died the moment she allowed her eyes to glance over at the pillow where his head might have been.

For the first time since receiving the news, the tears began to flow. The overwhelming sadness that she had stuffed inside her, welled up and came out of her mouth in a series of loud terrible sobs. He had come to her in her dream and told her he was OK and that she shouldn't worry about him. "I'm sorry Baby," he'd said. "I was angry, but it was an accident, I promise. Please don't imagine that it was your fault. It wasn't. It was meant to happen this way. I love you. Will you please forgive me?"

Verna was not only shocked but spooked. She didn't much believe in life after death and had never given any credence to stories of people being contacted by dead people. She had always dismissed such stories as wishful thinking.

But everything about her dream had seemed so real. She had heard his voice as clear as if he had been in the room. She saw him. She had felt him touch her head and stroke her hair. "It was just a dream," she said as if to reassure herself. "A nice dream, but a dream nevertheless. That's all there is to it."

With that, she threw back the covers, left her bed and went to the bathroom to wash away the tears. But as she looked in the mirror she leaned in to make a closer inspection of herself. Yes, she looked terrible but she was feeling better. Perhaps it was because she had finally allowed herself to cry, but it was more than that. She was more at peace. A weight had been lifted from her shoulders. It was almost as if she was now able to accept his death and be at peace with it. "This is weird. How can a dream change things so profoundly?" she thought. She got dressed, put on makeup and left the house.

# Chapter 5
# The Light Beckons

Joe was clearly impressed. "Nice work, pal! She was really hurting, but she got the message, I'm sure. What made you choose to enter her dream cycle rather than something more direct? I was rather looking forward to watching you create an image of yourself that she would perceive as you in bodily form."

"She would have totally freaked out if I'd done that," I explained. "She doesn't believe in this kind of stuff and she wouldn't have been happy to see me as a ghost. She can discount a dream and rationalize it away, at least initially. That way she can let it sink in slowly."

"Well, I saw her energy shift almost immediately, so I think she got it OK, even if she doesn't believe it yet. You did a great job. Not everyone is able to do that, I don't think, at least not to that degree. I'm too far gone now to do it myself, but quite honestly, I didn't have the desire. Not at first anyway. Then the window of opportunity passed. How about a drink?"

"No. I'm done with that," I replied curtly. "I just don't like the idea of occupying some other guy's body and sponging off him for something as worldly as a drink. I can easily see that might be just as addictive as being an alcoholic in real life."

"This IS real life," said Joe.

"No, it isn't," I countered. "It's between life — neither one thing nor the other. I don't want to stay in this never-never land. I want to go to the light and I want to go now."

"I've been waiting for you to say that." The voice belonged to a figure who had appeared out of nowhere and was now standing right in front of me. The voice was male but I couldn't see his face since it was shrouded in a copious hood that extended a long way in front of his face and left it completely in shadow.

"How do you do, I'm Death," he said in a matter-of-fact tone. "I'm here to escort you to the light." He had been addressing me directly, but turning to Joe he asked, "How about you? You too?"

Joe looked terrified. "Is it compulsory? I don't know that I am ready yet. I was planning to stay on down here for a while longer."

"No, of course it's not compulsory," Death replied somewhat reassuringly. "It's up to you, but there really isn't anything to be scared of. I know you've been told that God is very judgmental and likely to be angry if you have been bad in this lifetime, but it isn't true. All you will experience is overwhelming love. You will go through a life review so you get to see all the consequences of all your actions and decisions you made during your life, but that's just for your information and for your learning. You will not be criticized or judged in the least, and you certainly won't be punished."

"What about Hell?" asked Joe who was now shaking with fear.

"Doesn't exist," replied Death. "It's just a myth made up by people who want to control you by scaring the shit out of you. Hell is something you create here on Earth, Joe. You know, you've experienced some of it. But you're done with all that, unless you choose to stay, that is. It's up to you, though. Free will and all that."

"Come on Joe," I said persuasively, "Let's go together. No point in staying here. You'll just get more and more stuck in this plane and it will become more and more like the Hell you are so scared of. I'm sure it's going to be OK. Let's go."

Death waited patiently while Joe argued with himself internally. Finally he made the decision. "OK, but stick with me pal. I'm scared stiff."

"I will, I promise," I replied, noting that I too had a feeling not so much of fear but a mix of apprehension and delicious expectation.

# Chapter 6
# The Ride of My Death

WHOOSH! Suddenly we were both swept up and moving extremely fast up the tunnel of light. The light was blinding but it was at the same time warm and inviting. Joe and I were careering up the tunnel at what seemed like a breakneck speed. And, surprise, surprise, we were on a motorbike. A Harley Davidson no less, and I was at the handlebars. Joe was sitting behind me on the pillion seat holding on for dear life (in a manner of speaking only, of course) and I seemed to be driving. Whether I was actually in control of it is another matter but it felt like I was. It was good to be back on a bike again. Clearly Dr. Death had a sense of humor. He must have known I would want to go to Heaven on a Harley Davidson. Joe wasn't so happy about it, but he had decided to come along for the ride only at the last second, so he didn't get much choice.

It was not a long journey timewise. In fact, it seemed we were there almost as soon as we had started but the euphoria I was feeling as we approached the light was intense, more intense than any emotion I had ever experienced in my whole life. I began to realize that what I was feeling was in response to the incredible love that was emanating from the light ahead. Pure love such as I had never before experienced. Indescribable. There simply were no words adequate for it.

Barely discernible within the light, at what appeared to me to be center point of it, was what I can only describe as a *Presence*. It had no real form but it was unmistakably *there*. And it was both the source of the light and that from which all the love was emanating. Was it God? I didn't know. But it didn't matter, I just knew that I had come home.

"Welcome back!" said Harley. "Right on cue. We've been preparing for your return. The members of your soul group are here, waiting to see you, at least the ones who are back here already, plus other friends and relations you haven't seen in a while. But before we get you fully reunited with them, you need to do the life review. Are you ready?"

Suddenly it all became clear to me. I had been on a journey to the Earth plane and it had all been pre-planned. As my Angel of Incarnation, Harley had prepared me for that journey. He not only taught me what to expect but had set me up with a number of other souls who would play certain roles that would help me learn what I needed to learn during my lifetime.

As it all started to become clear, I saw the irony in the fact that during my incarnation I had always hankered after the Harley Davidson motorcycle. Was there a connection? Perhaps Harley had been a *biker* during one of his incarnations! He picked up on my thoughts.

"Did you like the Harley?" said Harley. "I thought I might as well bring you home in style. Motorcycles always were your soft spot, weren't they? Mine too as you might well imagine. That's the one thing I miss about being up here all the time. Every now and then I think about incarnating just to have a Harley and go on a few bike rides with all the other bikers, but then I think about all the other stuff that goes with it, and I make do with just my imagination. I've done all the incarnations I need to do. Now I just prepare souls like you to go do theirs."

The fact was that Harley was a very senior Angel of Incarnation and I recognized how lucky I was to have him as my mentor. He had such a wonderful compassionate presence and I felt safe with him. I found out later that Harley was responsible for having guided some very advanced souls in taking on some extremely difficult assignments. Like the one who became Hitler for example, and the one who incarnated as Saddam Hussein.

He also mentored the souls who became Martin Luther King and Nelson Mandela. And, would you believe it, George W. Bush. I couldn't help wondering why he was mentoring me. Hmmm.

"It was quite fitting that you should be killed on a motorcycle, don't you think? You gotta admit, the condition of your bike was not the best in the world to handle a bend at high speed, but it worked to our advantage actually. Seeing that it was your time, we saw to it that you would begin the journey really angry, knowing you always rode like a maniac when you were angry. Then we made that bend a little more slick than usual, and then pushed you to go a little faster than was prudent given the conditions. Worked like a dream didn't it?"

"I think I might have preferred a death with a slower pace to it," I replied, "so I could have said good-bye to a few people and put my affairs in order. Not to mention some forgiveness work that might have scored me a few points on my return here. I did manage to check in on my wife before I came back home, but even though she was asleep I could tell that she was in total shock and despair. I could do nothing for her. I couldn't comfort her. That's the worst part of a sudden death process, I feel."

"Yes, I know, but perhaps you might not be remembering quite yet, but that was the agreement," said Harley gently. "You and she agreed to do it this way so she would get to feel the sudden abandonment. She wanted to feel the pain of that kind of separation. Again, that's why the Harley Davidson was the perfect means to that end. Anyway, I think all this will begin to come clear as we go through your life review. At the moment you are still operating partly in human consciousness. It does take a little time to acclimatize to being back here. When you do, you will begin to recall all these agreements, so let's get into it."

Harley took me into another room which was square in shape but almost entirely featureless except for a very large white screen on one wall. All four walls were blue in color but even though they defined the space of the room, they didn't quite look like walls. Though solid in appearance and

33

totally opaque, there was nevertheless something insubstantial about them. They might have been nothing more than projected light for all I could make out. But they served the purpose of making a room and that's all that counted. I was later to be informed that it was always used for life reviews of those returning home after having completed their human journey.

There was a chair in the center of the room and a row of chairs set up as semicircle behind and around it. Harley motioned me to sit in the one central chair. I felt very exposed and rather nervous. I remembered the conversation I'd had with Joseph about being judged and condemned by God if you went towards the light, and I began to wonder whether he might not have been too wide of the mark. I had not been a paragon of virtue in my human life and was beginning to wonder whether there might be a price to pay after all.

"Don't worry," said Harley picking up on my fears. "It's not like that. We have no judgment here at all, and there is no right or wrong as far as we are concerned. But there are lessons to be learned all right. So it is helpful to see how exercising your free will at several points in your life either supported the unfoldment of your Divine Plan or interfered with it. That information will then be helpful to you in your next life. Let's bring in your soul group now, because they want to be part of this."

A door opened up in the far wall and in floated about ten souls who took their seats. They were so happy to see me and beamed love and support at me with such intensity that I literally felt lit up by their energy. All my fears evaporated immediately. As I looked at each one, the recognition was instantaneous and the heart connection automatic. The whole room now was bathed in love. I longed to get up and hug each one, but I sensed that it wouldn't be appropriate. Later.

"OK," began Harley. "Before we get into the specifics, let's just remind ourselves about why we choose to individuate and enter into the world of form and duality. What's the purpose? Why do we do it, and why do we do it over and over?"

"Thank you. I am still suffering from spiritual amnesia, so a brief recap will be very helpful," I said.

Harley continued. "The first and most important reason is that we incarnate in order to expand the consciousness of the Godhead, or Universal Intelligence. This is, of course, the very reason for our existence. Before we came onto the scene, there was no way for the Godhead to know itself as the Godhead, since it was beyond anything that could possibly describe it. So It created parts of Itself that could enter into existence and become manifest as a representation of Itself. Little bits of 'God Stuff' as they say — us.

"Our role was to expand our own awareness of Oneness (i.e. the quality of the Godhead Itself), by choosing to experience the opposite of it — separation. Being part of the Godhead, when we each expand our consciousness of Oneness, it affects the Godhead in the same way. A perfect arrangement, don't you agree?"

"It's a beautiful arrangement," I replied. "What an honor it is to serve the Godhead in this way. I am very proud to have been one of those to make the journey."

"Yes, it is an honor," replied Harley. "But, as you have discovered, being involved in this work is not without its challenges. Existence at that density feels very heavy and there is a great deal of limitation upon you all the time.

"Having a physical body, which is essential in order to feel the separation experience emotionally, is a huge strain on you. And without doubt, the emotional pain of separation can be very intense.

"So, when the time is right for you to make your journey into the human world, we first make sure your memory of this world is erased and then set it up for you to have plenty of opportunities to feel the pain of separation. This most commonly occurs within personal relationships but actually it occurs in all sorts of other situations too."

"Does one always have to suffer in order to experience separation?" I asked. "Must it always be painful?"

"It's always going to be painful, but let's be clear about this," replied Harley. "The pain of separation is not restricted to unpleasant or tragic events. It can be experienced in the most delicious of emotional experiences, like when looking into the eyes of the woman you love and seeing in that person such beauty and love that your greatest desire is to merge with her — to become one with her. But it is not possible to do that. So to be close but yet still separate from the person you love is painful. That's why people say that love hurts. You can merge emotionally and physically with someone, but you can't merge spiritually."

I looked over at the soul who had been Susan. She smiled knowingly. I had known deep love with her, but I knew what Harley meant. Even though we, as lovers and husband and wife, were as close as two people could be, we were still not One. Not really. We were still separate individuals and there was pain in that truth. Then, when death tore us apart, increasing the separation, the pain was excruciating.

"Do we choose how much pain we are willing to experience during our incarnation?" I asked.

"How much pain you get is a function of how much spiritual growth you are willing to have during that one lifetime. Some agree to experience more pain during a single incarnation simply in order to reduce the total number of incarnations necessary to complete their service. Others take it a little easier and spread it over several more lifetimes. We leave that up to you, because you do have free will, as you know. It is mostly decided ahead of time, but you can make adjustments as you go through the life experience."

"But how do you measure the pain of separation in a way that you'd know how much drama to create in any one lifetime?" I enquired.

"Good question," said Harley. "Clearly, we had to have some sort of scale against which to measure the pain of separation and to keep score. So, first we created a scale that begins at zero and goes down to minus 100. Zero equals Oneness such as we experience on this plane, while minus 100 equals unimaginable pain that only humans can feel.

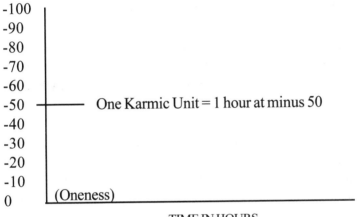

TIME IN HOURS

"Whereas we in this realm consistently exist at around zero with occasional dips to no more than minus three, it is impossible for any human to be above minus 10 at any point in their lifetime. A few even reach minus 90 but it is rare. The majority of people coast along at around minus 20, taking occasional dips to minus 70 or even minus 80 if things get really nasty."

Harley had projected the above diagram of the scale on the screen and was about to do his best to explain what a karmic unit was.

37

"A karmic unit is the measure of the pain of separation over time," said Harley. "The benchmark is that one karmic unit = 1 hour at minus 50 on the scale. Beyond that there is a very complicated mathematical formula that determines the length of time required to make a karmic unit at any other point on the scale and I can't even begin to tell you how that is calculated. The Godhead computer does it. The computer also keeps track of how many karmic units each soul is scoring throughout their life. That enables us to schedule their Awakening according to how many karmic units they signed up for ahead of time.

"That's when we would begin to send you messages to awaken. In your case, I think we sent you a book called *Radical Forgiveness*. That was the first thing we did, and it sparked the Awakening process in you, correct?"

"That's right. It did. I actually remember feeling that I had been asleep up to that point. Before that I was so sure of my world view and thought I had it all handled. Suddenly, a window opened, in came the light and my old world view started to melt away. It was quite alarming. But how many karmic units did I sign up for, Harley?"

Harley looked at his copy of my Akashic Record and replied. "Well, you signed up for 7,500 which was a lot, but you actually did more than that. As well as those situations you agreed to create ahead of time with your soul group, you used your free will to create some extra dramas as you went along. You did a total of 8,400."

At this point, the soul group burst into an enthusiastic round of applause. They were on their feet and began to sing and sway, clapping their hands in unison. Music began to flow from somewhere.

My former AA (Alcoholics Anonymous) sponsor spoke up. "Steve, you were hard to handle even during your Awakening phase. You were searching for Spirit all right, using spirits in some cases, but you created some real problems for yourself, if you recall. I worked hard to get you to take the healing road."

"Thanks," was all I could manage. As my sponsor, that man had been such a help to me during those bad days and I was feeling overwhelming gratitude towards him.

"And I was one of those problems, wasn't I?" volunteered a female soul who was standing behind me. I turned to face the soul who had seduced me into many sexual adventures and experiments with drugs.

"Yes, you were indeed," I responded. "But it was all pre-planned wasn't it? I remember setting it up with you before I went in."

"That's right," she replied, smiling widely. "It was fun for me, but painful for you, right?"

"Yes it was. I hated you for a long time after that."

"I know. But that was all part of the agreement too," she countered.

Harley tried to take back control. "It's not unusual to create a lot of drama during the Awakening phase. It can be a very tumultuous time because all that you have ever known is torn down, including your identity. If you are not your victim story, who are you? That's a real problem for a lot of people and it's not uncommon for people to take up their story again and go right back to Victimland. Back to sleep."

"But I was the one who got you to the point of Awakening, wasn't I, Steve?" The voice came from behind, but I knew instantly whose it was.

I turned around and again met the eyes of the soul I knew to have been Susan, my loving wife. At that moment the powerful feelings that welled up in me were almost overwhelming. Here was my love, the one who, as my wife and partner, had been the wellspring of my joy and happiness, while at the same time, because of her cruel and premature death, the source of so much of my pain. Four years of Hell from the day she was diagnosed with breast cancer to the day she died. I was devastated and

I came close to doing myself in on a number of occasions in the terrible months that followed. I didn't know who the hell I was at that point and rather than find out, I used alcohol, drugs and gratuitous sex to numb out the pain.

"It's so good to see you again, Steve," said Susan softly and lovingly. But even though I could feel her love intensely, it was not the same love as before. There was no pain in it. No neediness, no urgency, no sentimentality, no attachment, no baggage from the past. It was pure, fresh and immediate and carried no underlying meaning. As I opened to receive it, I felt my heart healed. The pain of separation evaporated immediately and all I could feel was pure love.

"Hello, Susan," I said dreamily, since it really did seem like a dream. I still was not fully acclimatized to the new vibration and part of me was still at the old frequency. "I have fantasized about this moment since the moment you died, always hoping that you would be here when I arrived. For a long time is was all that kept me from going out of my mind."

"I know how difficult it was for you," Susan replied, "But what you didn't know, of course, is that I was with you the whole while, supporting you through it, along with your Granddad. On each occasion that you came close to opting out, we sent you energy — enough energy just to keep you going. It wasn't your time yet."

"Was it your time to go exactly when you did, then?" I asked, even though I really knew the answer.

"Of course," Susan responded. "It was what we agreed up front, before we incarnated. You said you wanted to feel the pain of separation through having someone you deeply loved die just as the relationship was flowering. So, I volunteered to be that one. Are you beginning to remember that conversation now?"

It was still foggy, but my consciousness was beginning to clear in direct proportion, I suppose, to the increase in my vibratory rate. I was trying to pay close attention though and doing my best to activate my spiritual memory.

"The idea was that my early death would happen right when you had reached your karmic unit target. That would propel you into the dark night of your soul which in turn would force you to begin the search for your Satori," Susan further explained.

I turned back to Harley who had been quietly witnessing our reunion as husband and wife and the re-forming of the spiritual relationship we had before we incarnated. I looked at him quizzically. "Satori?"

"It's just another name for your Awakening," answered Harley. "A Satori moment is when you suddenly touch into the truth of what is and who you are. The process of Awakening can involve hundreds or even thousands of Satori moments, and may take many years."

My gaze went to the other souls in the room. I saw my mother, my father, my grandparents and even the soul who had played the role of the baby who died of SIDS. I wanted to go to each one as I had done with Susan, but Harley stopped me.

"You can connect with all these souls when the review is over," said Harley, rather sharply. "I don't want this to begin looking like a *This is Your Life* show."

Having wrested back control of the room, he turned to the white screen and projected a black line going from left to right, placed midway between top and bottom. "Let's plot this out now," he said, almost to himself.

41

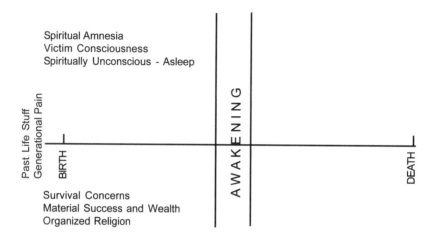

"This line represents your whole life," said Harley. "Birth to death. You agreed to accumulate 7,500 karmic units during the first half. This meant you needed a lot of drama early on in order to get such a high number of karmic units done by that time. So, to help you do it, we pulled together this wonderful soul group here and enrolled them into being the players in your life, who would provide opportunities for you feeling the pain of separation. They agreed to take on the roles of father, mother, wives, children and so on. They did a great job for you, didn't they?"

"Yes, they did," I replied, glancing around at everyone. They all smiled back and waved enthusiastically. They were so happy.

"But even before we got them involved, you already had about 250 karmic units in residual pain coming from a couple of past lives. We also looked at how much generational pain there was in your genetic makeup and found that you were carrying a lot of pain on behalf of your grandparents, especially those on your father's side. The Polish family.

"You carried pain for them three or four generations back, Steve, mostly about their separation from their land, their culture and their heritage through being invaded by hostile foreign powers — in modern times, first by the Germans and then by the Russians. That pain ran very deep in you Steve, but it gave you another 750 karmic units to begin with. That meant you began life, at birth, with 1,000 karmic units in the bank, so to speak.

"Even so, 6,500 was still a lot to get done in one lifetime so we needed to find you a couple of parents who would, first of all, tie into the generational pain that you already had downloaded, and secondly, treat you very badly more or less from the beginning.

"Obviously your father had to be Polish, so we chose to make your mother a German. We thought that would be an explosive mix and would ensure plenty of separation experiences for the whole family. We made Father a weak and feckless fellow as well as an alcoholic, and your mother a cruel, austere and controlling woman. He was a Catholic and she was a Lutheran. That made for plenty of conflict and dysfunction which is exactly what you needed to begin winning a reasonable numbers of karmic units in those early years."

The two souls who were my parents stepped forward and took a bow. "We gave you plenty of opportunity to feel the pain of separation, didn't we?" my mother said gleefully. "How else were you going to get that many karmic units in so short a time? You were the eldest so we had you all to ourselves in the early years, and what did we know about parenting? He being alcoholic and all, I hated him but I was scared of him too so I took it out on you. You got plenty of beatings from me and him." My father just sat there grinning.

"I guess it was all in the contract," I said. "You did a wonderful job and I am very grateful to you. I hope it wasn't too much of a strain on your spirit to be so ugly and mean."

"It was quite hard, actually," she replied. "But we got what we needed out of the contract too, you realize. It's always both ways, isn't it? You did what you did for us, and vice versa, so we're even."

Harley took over again. "Being the eldest of three, you took the brunt of most of the beatings which were frequent and severe. No need to go into details, but suffice it to say that in the first 13 years of your life, these two souls, playing the roles of mother and father, gave you the opportunity to accumulate about 1,000 ku in that time. That's a lot by any standard so those souls did you a great service. They were a good choice to play your parents."

I turned to look again at those two souls and felt extraordinarily loving towards them. They smiled back, returning the love. My father continued to wear that grin.

Harley continued the narrative as if they weren't there, speaking now about them not as the souls they were, but as the human parents they had been. "As you grew up the beatings lessened but after age 13 the separation took the form of a coldhearted and complete withdrawal of love by your parents. They rejected you and made you feel guilty because you wouldn't do the things they wanted you to do. They wanted you to study and become a lawyer or something like that, but it wasn't you. That added another 500 ku to your total. At age 18 you left and joined the Navy to get away from them.

"How about when I died? That was a traumatic experience for you, wasn't it, Steve? You were only eight years old and we were buddies, you and I."

The soul who had just spoken up was my grandfather on the Polish side of the family. He was right. We were very close indeed. He was the one person in the world I could talk to. He understood me and would talk with me for hours and show me how things worked. He understood that I was not treated well by my mother and father, his own son, but nothing was ever said about it, at least not directly. It was just an understanding between the two of us and that made it bearable. When he died, I was devastated. It was like my whole world fell apart.

"Yes, we were, Granddad," I responded. Tears were welling up in me as I reconnected energetically with this beautiful soul. "I missed you so much when you died. I guess you knew that, right?"

"Of course. And I was beside you all the way through the rest of your life. When Susan returned home, we teamed up on a number of occasions to pull you through some hard times, but I was there for you in the early days too.

"You know, it's hard for us up here to resist rescuing souls doing their journey down there. I saw you going through terrible pain and I desperately wanted to find a way to spare you the suffering. But I just had to remember that the pain is what you signed up for and needed to experience. So it was all perfect. Nevertheless, I did my best to provide whatever comfort I could."

"Thank you." I said.

Harley interjected. "The pain of that separation from your grandfather and the wound that it created in you, was so severe it earned you another 500 karmic units. That wound was to be repeated a number of times in your life."

"My life pattern?"

"Yes. We tend to arrange lives in patterns because doing the same pain over and over in a sequence with a lot of different people not only leverages the pain, but it gets your attention when you begin the Awakening. Actually seeing the patterns in your life is one of those Satori moments I was talking about."

"I tended to repeat the wound about every ten years or so," I offered. "It was a real Satori moment for me when I saw the pattern." I used the screen to show my patterns on a timeline.

45

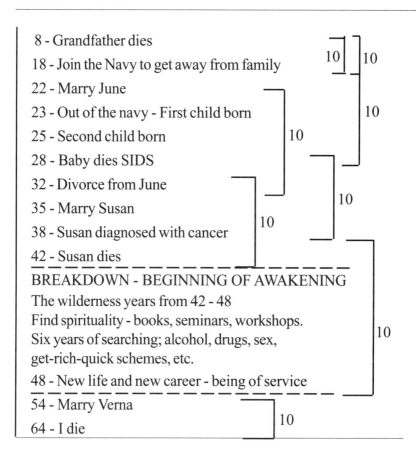

8 - Grandfather dies

18 - Join the Navy to get away from family

22 - Marry June

23 - Out of the navy - First child born

25 - Second child born

28 - Baby dies SIDS

32 - Divorce from June

35 - Marry Susan

38 - Susan diagnosed with cancer

42 - Susan dies

BREAKDOWN - BEGINNING OF AWAKENING

The wilderness years from 42 - 48

Find spirituality - books, seminars, workshops.

Six years of searching; alcohol, drugs, sex, get-rich-quick schemes, etc.

48 - New life and new career - being of service

54 - Marry Verna

64 - I die

"I leave home at 18. At 28 my baby dies. At 38 Susan is diagnosed with cancer. At 48 I begin a new life and a new career. That's one series of 10 ending with a good thing — a healing. In between are another ten where I divorce June when I am 32 and Susan dies when I am 42. Finally, I marry Verna when I am 54 and I die at 64. Wow!"

"It certainly looks like ten is your number doesn't it?" observed Harley. "By the time you were 20, you'd already accumulated 2,000 ku. The death of your new baby was a huge blow to you and, combined with what it did to ruin your marriage and create the divorce, that got you another 1,500 ku. A total of 3,500 and you were only 32. Not too bad really."

Harley then projected a blue line above the black line that made peaks and troughs. The peaks represented the moments of maximum pain. Under the black line he projected a red line that rose and fell as a mirror image to the blue one, indicating the amount of repressed pain associated with each peak experience. Repressing or suppressing the pain serves the purpose of leveraging it. The more it is repressed the more pain it creates over time and therefore the more karmic units it earns.

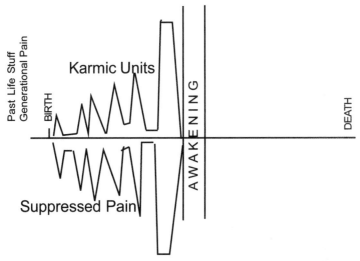

"But there being still a long way to go to reach the target, when you were 38 we sent you Susan. This was going to be the big one that would earn you a whole bunch of karmic units, we thought, and hopefully propel you into breakdown mode, right on cue for the first Satori in your early 40s.

"It worked like a charm. You both fell very deeply in love, so much so that when she got cancer and died after four years from the date of diagnosis, with you taking care of her for most of that time and watching her waste away and suffer horribly, the pain was unbearable.

"At the time, we thought we might have overdone it and that you might choose to opt out. But you didn't. The group up here worked with you to keep you in the process and to help you through it all. Anyway, it earned you the full remaining 3,500 ku. And that meant you could then begin the Awakening."

"You mentioned earlier that I earned some extra karmic units beyond the 7,500 I volunteered for," I interjected. "When did I earn those?"

"You racked up another 1,000 units during the Awakening phase," replied Harley. "As your AA sponsor indicated earlier, your breakdown experience resulted in a lot of the usual destructive behavior that sometimes accompanies the beginning part of the Awakening. Those led to some very painful experiences, so you got credit for those too."

Harley then switched gears and put a question to me. "So, Steve, once you began your Awakening, tell us what changed for you? What shifted?"

"Well," I began. "As you know I reacted badly at first because I found myself without a compass. The world that I knew and which, up to then, had defined me had disintegrated. I drank more heavily and became very self-destructive for a while. But after about six months, something happened to me internally. It was as if a switch had been thrown. I was feeling an inner peace I had never known before. I stopped drinking altogether and started to put my life back together. I didn't need alcohol anymore because I had given myself permission to feel my pain. I didn't need to medicate it anymore. That was a tremendous relief. All my addictions went away.

"The more I studied the new spirituality, the more I felt the need to do something meaningful with my life. I had completely lost interest in my real estate business. It was still giving me a small income, but I did no more buying and selling. Just making money for the sake of making money became meaningless to me and I was looking for a way to make a difference.

"I wanted a purpose to my life. I felt the need to be of service to others in some way. So I sold some of my holdings, mostly to the people living in them, for a very low price, and used the money to enroll in a training program to become a life coach. I got qualified in that and I did very well at it. But it still wasn't enough. I wanted to be able to provide some kind of spiritual element to the life coaching process. It wasn't just me; my clients wanted it too. So I bought the training program that would certify me as a Radical Forgiveness Coach. It was exactly what I needed and my business took off. I loved the work.

"But even though the career change was a big deal, what was really amazing was the change in me. I was happier than I had ever been and I stopped seeing myself as a victim. I become more conscious of my behavior and would catch myself whenever I started to lay blame, justify and judge. Not that I didn't do those things, but at least I could observe myself doing them and could then choose to stop doing them. The one thing that didn't stop, though, was my anger. In spite of doing countless Radical Forgiveness worksheets, I remained mad that Susan had been taken from me and I couldn't seem to get beyond the grief. But at least I was allowing myself to feel it and not medicating it. I let myself have the grief and the anger. I stayed present to it."

"This might be a good moment to begin completing the other side of the diagram," said Harley. "You have just accurately described what generally happens to people after the Awakening. Let me summarize it for everyone.

"First of all, almost everyone notices a shift in priorities. Whereas before they were focused on survival, security, material success and money, they find themselves trusting more in Spirit, being more in the moment and wanting to be of service to others in some way. That obviously happened to you, right?"

"Yes, it did," I concurred. "That describes my shift very accurately."

"Secondly, they become self-aware and develop what we call the Observer. This is the part of you that, in a very non-judgmental way, is able to see when you begin to go back into Victimland. It keeps you conscious and pulls you out of the funk very quickly. So, instead of staying mired in

49

judgment and resentment for days, months or even years like you would have before the Awakening, you move through it quickly and easily. After all, at this point no one is trying to win karmic units from the dramas. So, this shows up on the diagram as a number of events causing smaller emotional responses than they would have previously and they last for only a very short while. Would you say that was true for you?"

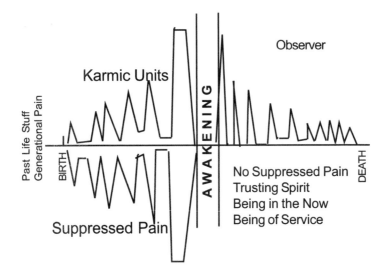

"Absolutely," I replied. "I always had a short fuse and even then I still got activated easily, but it was over in a few moments. I also stayed present to my feelings instead of suppressing or repressing them and didn't judge them.

"I have to confess though, that my anger did return when I married Verna, and I did tend to go back to Victimland for some long periods of time.

"I was four years into my new career when I married her and she became my rock. She was very spiritual and gave me space to be me. But she had her own baggage too and after we had been married for about six months, it began to trigger my anger, quite frequently in fact. Because we had the Radical Forgiveness technology, we were able to work through it quickly, but my outbursts upset her a lot."

"I know that," said Harley who had been listening intently to me and watching my energy. "After you had awakened at least to a fair degree, we put you together with Verna so you would activate some of her stuff.

"It was another way to be of service, soul to soul. We knew she would get attached to you and feel it to be a terrible loss when we took you back home, but again it was agreed up front. She needed that for her own growth. You'll see that when she gets back up here and does her review. You'll be here to be reunited with her and she will bless you for all that you did that seemed to be so bad at the time.

"So don't judge yourself too harshly. On the other hand, see what there is yet to learn about how you dealt with your anger and grief. Why couldn't you release it? What was the payoff for holding onto it? Think about it for you may want to deal with this before you do your next incarnation — if indeed you have one."

"What do you mean, if I have one?" I said, jumping on his last words. "Are you saying I have finished? Am I off the wheel?"

"Not really," replied Harley, deflecting my question and obviously regretting having made that caveat. "None of us are really finished in that sense. We are all capable of going in again when needed, even for just a few moments.

"So, while we may have been rotated out of continuous incarnation, we are all in the *Reserve,* so to speak, ready to respond to any need if required. The last time I had to go in and do some heavy duty rescue work was during the Cuban Missile Crisis. The mad men in the Kremlin and the trigger-happy generals in the Pentagon were about to turn the planet into a nuclear wasteland. Free will is one thing, but we weren't going to let that happen. So a lot of us senior angels went in and stopped it. It was a close call though."

I was not going to let him sidetrack me. I needed to know for sure whether I was going to reincarnate again as another human being somewhere on

Earth, even if it was to continue working through my anger and learning acceptance. That did seem to be the lesson I hadn't yet mastered. "So, what IS next for me, Harley?"

"I don't know yet," replied Harley, diplomatically. "I need to check your Akashic Record some more before I decide. I'll get back to you later. In the meantime, go party with your soul group. They've been waiting a long time for this moment to be with you, and you have earned it too. Have fun. I'll see you tomorrow."

With that, Harley vanished. So did the walls and the screen. Suddenly I was with my soul group in a beautiful landscape comprising rolling green pastures with cool rivers meandering through them, brightly colored flowers in full bloom, birds singing in the trees, swallows sweeping and diving all around us. It was blissful.

We sat there for many delightful hours discussing our journey and the parts we each had played for each other. I was still having to be reminded how we had made our soul contracts with each other. We recalled each of our pre-incarnation meetings and how we had to persuade each other to be the *bad* person for us in all sorts of different circumstances. We had done it for each other many times and in many different lifetimes. It all seemed so amusing now. We laughed and sang songs together for hours.

Suddenly I noticed someone coming towards us. He was waving. It was Joe! I had been wondering how he was doing and now here he was. I was so pleased to see my old friend again. "How are you Joe? It's great to see you. Have you had your review?"

"You bet I have," replied Joe. "I catch the next train out to Hell first thing in the morning."

We all fell quiet and stared at him blankly.

"Just kidding, guys," he laughed. "Of course the review went well. You were right all along. No need to have worried about it in the least. Everyone was very understanding about my failings and peccadilloes, but once I owned up to it all they showed me how it was all perfect in terms of the big picture. How was your review? Did it go all right?"

"Oh yes, very much so. It's been wonderful," I replied, "Do you have your next assignment?" I asked, not so much out of concern for his future, but in the hope that there may be a clue in his answer that might tell me more about mine.

"I have." said Joe. "My soul group had been arranging it all the while I had been hanging around that darn shrine my family put by the side of the road. I must have been there for much longer than I thought. Thank goodness you came along and dragged me along with you. I might still be there now if it weren't for you, pal. Thanks."

"So what is your new incarnation going to be like?" I asked impatiently. "Will you be male or female?"

"Oh, male again. I'm going to be born into a family in the Middle East. Iraq, I think. I was a real hawk about that war in my last incarnation and rooted hard for it. I thought Bush was a real hero, at first anyway. I was always for strong military action against the *enemy* and if I had been in charge I would probably have thrown a tactical nuclear bomb on the whole region. That was my feeling at least, so I guess this lifetime will be about balancing that karma. I'm to be a Muslim and in all likelihood will probably become a terrorist. That being the case, it might be quite a short incarnation so I will have a lot to do to get my quota of karmic units done in that short a time. I didn't really awaken before my death this time around, so maybe I won't next time either. On the other hand, I might. I'm not signing up to make more than a thousand karmic units, so maybe I will."

"Well, good luck."

53

"Maybe I'll see you in Iraq," he said, only half in jest. "You could get the same assignment, if only to drag my sorry terrorist ass back up here like you did last time."

Joe strolled off laughing. I wasn't much amused by his last minute joke, if only because it reminded me that my fate was still in the balance. I said to myself, "Please let it not be in Iraq with Joe!"

# Chapter 7
# The Big Mission

The next day, I was summoned to Harley's office. I entered with Joe's words about an Iraq assignment ringing in my ears, wondering what my fate might be. To counter that fear, I also had in mind what Harley had hinted at when he raised some doubt as to whether I would have an incarnation or not.

"Good morning, Steve," said Harley in a voice that immediately set a bright tone to the encounter. "How are you feeling today, having been back home for just a short while?"

"I'm still getting used to it," I replied. "I am still thinking in time and space terms rather than just being in the eternal now, but I am working on that. My spiritual amnesia is wearing off and my recall of the agreements I made with the souls in my group has improved. My get-together with them all yesterday was very helpful in that regard. We had a wonderful time going over everything."

"And what about your awareness of Oneness?" Harley asked.

"It's absolutely amazing," I replied excitedly. "I can hardly believe what a difference having the experience of the opposite of Oneness has made, not only to my awareness of Oneness but my appreciation of it. I am already many thousand times more conscious of it now and the expansion is still occurring, exponentially I think."

"Well, that's good," said Harley. "That expansion also contributes to the expansion of the mind of the Godhead, as you know — the very purpose for our existence. And that brings me to what I want to talk to you about, Steve, and why I have asked you to come here.

"Yesterday — yes, I am still speaking as if time is real, but only because I can see that you are still thinking in these terms — I hinted that you might not need to do any further incarnations. You have, after all, completed more than a thousand of them. I have consulted with Ones at the next level and it has been decided that you will not do an incarnation again this time."

My relief was palpable, so much so that Harley picked up on it immediately. "Wait until you hear what you are going to do," said Harley. "It might make going to Iraq to be a terrorist look like a walk in the park."

I just swallowed hard and said nothing. Harley continued.

"You are to be given the job of orchestrating from up here, the biggest shift in consciousness that has occurred since humans came on the planet. Before I tell you more, let me give you some background, Steve.

"This whole experiment began with the Big Bang. Before that there was only consciousness — pure potential. The Big Bang occurred and the entire Universe manifested when consciousness created the very first thought, which was: 'What if there is something else?' This creation process has been going on ever since at an ever accelerating pace.

"However, there came a point in the expansion of the consciousness of Universal Intelligence where It needed to know Itself in order to become the Godhead. However, since Universal Intelligence could not experience Itself as Itself, It created us so It could experience Itself vicariously through us. We talked about this yesterday prior to the review, remember?"

"I do," I replied.

"Well, the fact is the experiment is soon to be over. A sufficient number of souls have made the human journey enough times to have expanded the mind of the Godhead to the extent that It is now totally Self-aware. Which means that there will be no further need for anyone to experience separation. Wars, conflict, strife, hunger, discrimination, torture, abuse, pain and suffering will be no more."

"Great! Does that mean the end of planet Earth and life in a human body?" I asked.

"Not at all," said Harley. "The Godhead sees the culmination of the experiment as being the merging of both worlds — the World of Spirit and the World of Humanity — into one. That is, to have Heaven-on-Earth. That way Universal Intelligence can experience Itself not just as a thought, which is how It has experienced Itself up to now, but as a feeling experience as well. That means we all get to have bodies through which to feel the experience of existence while at the same time feeling the bliss of total Oneness."

"So is the Godhead soon to make a declaration that the experiment is over and to announce the formation of Heaven-on-Earth? And will all the souls currently down there in a body be brought back home?" I asked, hoping that the task I was about to be given was to be easily accomplished.

"No," replied Harley emphatically. "Even though It has the power to do anything It wants, Universal Intelligence never creates outcomes by decree. It could create Heaven-on-Earth in a second if It wanted to. With Universal Intelligence, the name of the game is transformation, which means that it's the process that counts.

"What Universal Intelligence wants is for each country to go through the same kind of Awakening each human being goes through, with America being the first to go. America will then lead the world in taking the whole human race through the Awakening process. That's when we shall have

Heaven-on-Earth, not before. The human race has to choose it. Free will — remember?

"Your job will be to orchestrate this mass transformation from up here as leader of the soul group that will coordinate everything. This group will communicate directly with the very large contingent of souls we have already sent in to prepare the way. These are those souls known as the Indigos and the Crystals. They are different from all other humans who have gone before because they are not forgetting who they are. They are, in effect, already Awakened."

I was beginning to feel extremely nervous. This sounded like a very big assignment to me and I couldn't help feeling fearful that I might not be up to the job. "What will I be expected to do, Harley?" I asked nervously.

"The plan is to set America up for its Awakening first. You will be responsible for making that happen. Now, as you know, and have experienced yourself, it is always the case that just before our Awakening, we experience a complete breakdown. The fact is that it's only through breakdown that we achieve the breakthrough necessary to create the Awakening. Therefore it is necessary to create circumstances in America that will lead to a dramatic social, economic and political breakdown.

This plan has already been set in motion. We have sent in a highly trained soul whose mission it is to become the president of the United States and to take the country at least through the start of the breakdown process. His name is Jack Barber. He may change his name at some point during the process or he may just do a short cut and become a *walk-in.*

"However he chooses to do that, your job is to guide both him and the presidents that will follow him to make sure that the breakdown occurs as planned. The true breakdown is scheduled to begin happening in a serious way around 2012 and to be fully complete around 2028. At some moment during that period America's Awakening will occur.

"I personally prepared Jack for the job and he is down there now, along with a few other souls out of his group that have roles to play. One played Saddam Hussein — he's now back home — one plays Osama Bin Laden, another plays the Iranian president and so on. You can read the entire script of my conversations with him made during his preparation phase by downloading from the Godhead website, the e-book we made of it.* It is also available on CD if you would prefer to listen to it.** It explains the whole strategy, so I strongly suggest that you read the text and listen to the CD.

"It also tells the existing human population how they can make the transition from breakdown to breakthrough without it involving as much chaos and suffering as it might if they resist the process and go kicking and screaming. Basically, what they have to do to prevent it from being a cataclysmic event is to get ahead of the process and do a lot of spiritual work that will change the energy. One way is to do a lot of Radical Forgiveness work on themselves and on the world leaders.***

"So go now and read up on it, Steve. This is a huge assignment but I think you can handle it."

With that, Harley disappeared. Totally stunned and out of body, I made my way to the library to get that e-book and the CD. I almost wished I was going to Iraq with Joe. But then again, I might be. Could it be that the Iraq war is Phase One of the breakdown? I was soon to find out.

---

* The story about Jack Barber's preparation is contained in the book, "A Radical Incarnation," by Colin Tipping. Refer to the Appendix, Page 192, for details.

** The same story (abridged) is offered on CD and can be obtained from the web site, www.radicalforgiveness.com. See Appendix for details.

*** Go to the web site, www.radicalforgiveness to download worksheets and other tools. See Appendix for details.

# Preface to Part Two

# What I Will Say About Me
# When I'm Gone

In the Introduction to this book I listed some of the most important questions we can ask ourselves: Who am I? What am I? Why am I here? And, what is the meaning of my life? We might also add: What is my mission? What is my purpose? What is the right action for me to take now?

Through reading the story in Part One, you may already have found some answers to those questions, at least in general terms. Hopefully you found some resonance with some of them, notwithstanding the fact that you will have realized that they are grounded in my Radical Forgiveness myth.

For those who are not altogether familiar with the concept of Radical Forgiveness I have, in Part Four, Page 159, written the basic underlying assumptions of the Radical Forgiveness myth and explained some of the tools associated with it that make it easy and simple to achieve.

However, I expect you have gathered from Steve Parker's life review story that the fundamental idea is that there are no accidents and everything happens for a reason. It is suggested that life is not just a set of random events but a carefully orchestrated, highly complicated, and to a large degree predestined outplaying of a Divine plan — plus some free will to do things our own way as we go. We are Spiritual beings who have chosen to make a journey into the realm of physical form and duality in order to expand the consciousness of Universal Intelligence and learn certain lessons for our soul growth.

It also suggests that we incarnate, having agreed beforehand with other souls to act out certain scenarios that will give us the lessons we want, while we do the same for them. These souls often appear as our enemies in our human lives but they are really our most loving assistants and teachers. As Ram Dass put it, "Planet Earth is the school; life is the curriculum and our fellow human beings are our teachers."

Our own Spiritual Intelligence, it is proposed, also recognizes opportunities for growth in situations that spontaneously occur during the life experience and turns them into useful learning experiences. These may look like random events such as accidents, misfortunes, bad luck, crimes committed against you and so on, but they are not. They are self-created opportunities to feel the pain of separation which is, of course, the whole idea. That the experiencing of such pain is the purpose of our journey is well set out in the story.

The important thing to understand from where you are standing now, however, is that you don't have to believe a word of the Radical Forgiveness myth for it to work for you. All that is required is a small amount of willingness to at least be open to the possibility that there is a grain of truth in it, and to try using the simple tools that the technology of Radical Forgiveness provides — then see what happens. Skepticism is a healthy attitude with which to approach Radical Forgiveness and will not prevent you getting worthwhile benefits from the process. These can be substantial and are often experienced in ways that are little short of miraculous.

The explanations embedded in the story about death, the afterlife and the meaning of our lives, are by no means exclusively mine and certainly not new. But are they the truth? I doubt that they are even close. None of us really knows the truth — we are not yet privy to the Spiritual Big Picture. But I have spun these ideas in my own way consistent with the Radical Forgiveness concept and they seem reasonable assumptions to me at this time, given what we know and what we intuitively feel about our spiritual lives.

Experience has also shown me that these ideas have a utility in that they impart a certain resonance which is of a positive and healthy nature. I have found that when we allow ourselves to be in the vibration that these notions create in and around us, life works better, we feel more loving and compassionate towards each other and we feel more peaceful. We also behave with more humility, compassion and tolerance and are more likely to see the best rather than the worst in people. That can't be bad.

Nevertheless, I ask you not to blindly accept them as the truth, which they are probably not, but to *play with them* in this forthcoming section and see what happens. I say play with them because it's one thing to entertain these ideas as an intellectual exercise, but quite another to get them integrated into your whole beingness so they give real meaning and direction to your life.

This is precisely my purpose for writing this book and my goal for all who might read it and do the work contained herein. Just as I used the device of *story* to give a generalized meaning to life and death, seen through the Radical Forgiveness perspective, I am suggesting that you now use the same template to find the meaning in your own life and to do it using the worksheets and exercises provided in the sections that follow. They are designed to provide you with a basic framework for conducting this exciting research into your own life and what it really means.

In other words, I am going to suggest that you imagine yourself having just gone through the death experience and are going through the life review process just like Steve did. The effect of doing this will be twofold. First, it will put into perspective everything that has ever happened to you and, second, will provide you with a wonderful road map that will serve you for the rest of your journey on this planet.

You might at this point be wondering where you might be on this journey. The obvious question to ask is: "Have I Awakened yet?"

Well, let me settle this question for you. It is my conviction that you would not have even picked up this book in the first place, let alone got this far, had you not reached the point of being either close to, in the middle of, or in the later stages of the Awakening process.

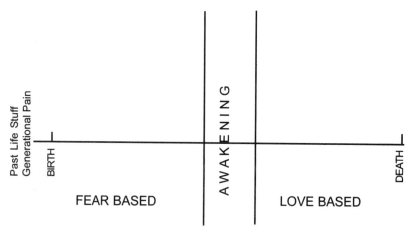

Referencing back to where in the story you first saw this diagram, you might recall that the period leading up to the Awakening is characterized as a period in one's actual human life in which one is spiritually unconscious, unaware of spiritual reality beyond the superficial, or that which is given them from society or institutions. The focus is on survival, making money, creating material success, accumulating wealth, controlling as many aspects of life as possible and seeing life as a zero sum game. In short, one is committed to victim consciousness and acting from a world view that supports that way of thinking. It is a fear based way of being.

From the spiritual standpoint, this is entirely purposeful because this is the time during which our Spiritual Intelligence sets us up for all our separation experiences — the ones that will enable us to accumulate the amount of *karmic units* we pledged to gather prior to our Awakening. This absolutely requires that we be mostly asleep to, and unaware of, the spiritual reality we speak of here in this book. At this stage we are all EGO.

Without victim consciousness our life experiences would not give us the amount of *separation angst* we wanted and therefore very few karmic units in the bank. If we were constantly recognizing the spiritual perfection in everything that was occurring and actually seeing our enemies as our teachers, we would gain little from the experience, and that wouldn't be helpful. We might just as well have stayed *home*.

This book may or may not actually be your first Satori, but the fact that it came into your possession at all is no accident. This is no less true for the other things that have occurred in your life to bring you to the point of Awakening. There have been many Satoris and there will no doubt be more as you continue your spiritual journey.

Typically, when people are at the breakdown stage, which you now know occurs just before the Awakening phase, their first Satori is a book like my own book, *Radical Forgiveness, Making Room for the Miracle*, or others like *Conversations With God* by Neale Donald Walsch. It's going back a bit now but for many people the book, *You Can Heal Your Life*, by Louise Hay was the Satori that opened the door. For others it might have been a workshop given by someone who was already Awakened, as it was for me with Arnold Patent.

However, since this book is a fairly advanced piece of spiritual technology, it is my guess that you may have read these books already, as well as many others and have attended plenty of workshops. I feel it likely therefore you are at least a fair way into the Awakening phase at this point in time. I may be wrong about that, of course, but I still don't believe I am in error in saying that you would not be reading this book if you were still unconscious. It wouldn't be serving you if you were.

So, having said all that and assuming you are in agreement with my assessment, put a marker↓ on the timeline where you think you are now. Under the line, mark your age.

**Note:** Even if you agree with me that you are likely to be either about to reach the point of Awakening, or some way into it or even beyond it, this does not necessarily mean you are at the halfway point in your life. I only suggest that it is *normal* for the Awakening to occur around that time on the basis of my observation of those who attend my Radical Forgiveness workshops. They are usually at the Awaking point for the reasons I have described above and tend to be over 40 and, not infrequently, in their late 50s and 60s.

It also makes sense that 40 or so years hanging out in *Victimland* might be necessary in order to experience a sufficient amount of separation angst — that is, unless they are coming in to work on past life or generational pain, in which case they might not need to create as much drama in their current life to satisfy their needs. Carl Jung put it this way: "We spend the first half of our lives integrating the Ego, and the second half of our lives disintegrating the Ego."

What follows is a series of *Research Assignments,* the purpose of which is to provide relevant data about your life with which to begin constructing your life review — from present time all the way back to birth and even past lives.

Then, in Part Three you will be invited to *look forward* from the point at which you Awakened, looking at what might be necessary to consolidate the shift and stay awake. You will then be able to create a road map for the future consistent with your mission and purpose.

I think you will find this to be an amazing journey of self-discovery and a profoundly life-changing process. Get ready for the ride of your life — to heaven on a Harley!

# PART TWO

## Constructing Your Own Life Review
### *(Research Assignments)*

# Past Life Bleedthrough

I seldom recommend that people spend much time on this part of the research. My feeling about this in general is that dealing with what we have created in this lifetime is difficult enough without adding to the analysis the kind of complication that past lives introduce.

I say this because usually people have only sketchy information at best about what might have happened in past lives and it is usually very unreliable and unverifiable. Typically people have learned it from someone who claimed to *know* such things or channeled the information during a so-called past life reading. Another way people access the information is by having a past life regression through hypnosis.

I am skeptical about most forms of past life therapy because I have seen so many people take it as gospel and then use it as a way to further justify their victimhood. I say this even though I have been a hypnotherapist and conducted many past life regressions myself. Yes, there are times when information like this does ring true, but whether it is truly accurate past life information, I am not at all sure.

Having said that though, if you feel that one or more past lives have had a strong influence on your current life, then by all means include it in your research and analysis. Just be respectful of it. It has been my experience that people who do report significant past life bleedthrough usually cite the manner in which they died in that past life as the issue bleeding through into this life. For example, I did have a client who was terrified of fire and though she had had some bad experiences with fires in this life, had experienced her terror before those fires occurred. When we did the regression, she experienced and relived being burned to death in a house fire. It was very traumatizing for her to go back through it, but afterwards she was free of her phobia about fire.

**Tasks:**

**1.** Make a note of any past life information that is meaningful to you.

**2.** Determine in each case whether it is, in fact, bleeding through into this life and journal the ways it is affecting your current life.

**3.** How many karmic units do you think should be credited to you for this *pain.* _____?

# Generational Pain

How much of the pain you are carrying around do you think might be pain that you have taken on from your parents, your grandparents and their forebears some generations back? This is a very important question for you to try to answer, because it could easily be the key that unlocks a tremendous amount of unresolved pain.

In my Radical Forgiveness workshops I am finding more and more that the pain being experienced by a high proportion of the participants is generational in nature. It may go back many generations and typically it gets passed on to the next. The most obvious example is the pain of slavery. African Americans are still carrying this pain forward from generation to generation. Another example is the holocaust. When all the holocaust survivors are dead, you can be sure that the Jews will carry the pain of that experience forward for many generations to come as well.

While I assert in this book that we incarnate with the intention of experiencing the pain of separation, I don't think the plan demands that we be masochistic about it. There isn't much mileage (or many karmic units) to be gained by hanging on to repressed pain for years on end or by passing it from one generation to the next. Better that we go through it in the present moment, experience it fully and then move on to the next thing. Repressing it and then passing it on to our children is not earning us many karmic units and it turns out to be a very weak learning experience for whomever has to work it through on our behalf in a future generation. For them it's a distraction from their own journey, they don't earn many karmic units and for us it's nothing less than a copout.

Many people tend to carry one or both of their parents' pain — their disappointments, their fears, their hurts, their sadness, anger and so on.

Not infrequently, it's a grandparent's pain as well — either the same pain they passed on to his or her children, or something completely different that the child has picked up on.

The transference usually happens when a child becomes aware of or witnesses his or her parent's pain. Since the child's life force energy is often stronger and more pure than the adult's, especially one who has been dragged down by life, the child unconsciously *volunteers* to carry the energy of the pain in order to support the parent through a difficult time. But because there is often negative energy associated with the pain, it is repressed by the child as well as the parent. The result is that he or she becomes the permanent surrogate carrier of that pain and the parent never gets it back.

This is good for neither the adult nor the child. The adult does not get the true benefit of the experience because the pain has been appropriated by the child, not just for a brief period but permanently. Paradoxically the child has damaged the parent because the parent is deprived of the very pain he or she was trying to work through and learn from. And the child gets no real learning value from it because it is not his own pain. In fact, it might prevent him from getting the most learning from his own self-created experiences and, as a result, delay his Awakening.

So, I tell the person to give the pain back, no matter whether the parent is dead or not. I tell them that they have no right to it because it is not their own and that they are actually depriving their parents of the spiritual growth that was inherent in their dealing with the pain themselves.

Some interesting scientific evidence has recently come out that supports the idea that emotions get carried forward in the *epigenome*, a layer of biochemical reactions that turns genes on and off. It used to be thought that DNA controlled destiny but this research is showing that experiences, including emotional experiences, are passed from generation to generation. The epigenome can change according to an individual's physical or emotional environment.

This tendency to carry other people's pain may express itself in adulthood as co-dependence. One of the features of co-dependency is a tendency towards wanting to *rescue* people, the result of which is the same as taking on other people's pain. Resist the temptation!

**Tasks:**

**1.** Name all the people in your family of origin back at least to grandparents on both sides if possible.

**2.** Against each name, make a note of the emotional issues that you feel might have dominated their lives.

**3.** Ask yourself whether any of those emotional issues have shown up in some form or another in your own life. Make a particular note as to whether a pattern has emerged in your own life around any one of these issues.

Mother _____

_____

_____

_____

Father _____

_____

_____

_____

_____

Siblings _____

_____

_____

_____

_____

_____

_____

Maternal Grandmother _____

_____

_____

_____

Maternal Grandfather _____

_____

_____

_____

Paternal Grandmother _____

_____

_____

_____

Paternal Grandfather _____

_____

_____

_____

Notes to Myself _____

_____

_____

Research Assignment #3

# 7,500 Karmic Units

Since we are using a template based on Steve Parker's life review, let's imagine that prior to your incarnation, in consultation with Harley (assuming that he was your Angel of Incarnation too), you also decided that you would set your goal of accumulating 7,500 karmic units before waking up. Like Steve and many others like him, you might have continued creating more drama and gathering more karmic units even during the Awakening phase, but that's a number you can adjust for yourself later as you look at where you are in relation to this phase.

[**Recap:** A Karmic Unit is the measure of the pain of separation over time, the benchmark being one karmic unit = one hour at minus 50 on a pain scale between zero and minus 100. Minus 100 is the most pain that any human being could endure.]

So, working on the basis that 7,500 ku was your goal, and assuming that you have already achieved it since you wouldn't be reading this book if you hadn't, you might just pencil in a number for both past life pain and generational pain. You may want to adjust it later as you research your life from birth onwards, but at least it will be a starting point.

**Past Life Pain Brought Forward:**

_____


**Generational Pain Brought Forward:**

_____

Research Assignment #4

# Your Emotional History

Having researched the pain you may have brought forward into your present life from past generations and past life experiences, your next step is to list as many significant emotional events as possible that have occurred to you since the day you were born up to present time.

As you list each event, make an assessment of how painful it was at the time it occurred and pencil in an estimate of how many karmic units you accumulated as a result of going through the pain of it. (Use pencil because you may keep changing your assessment of each experience relative to others as you proceed through the whole research process in order to end up with a total of 7,500.)

It is not always easy to remember everything that happened to you, especially if what happened was unpleasant, frightening, shameful or in some other way traumatic. That's because it is our nature to defend against pain by blocking our memory of unpleasant experiences. It enables us to cope and to go on with life. Another way is to suppress the memory by never talking about it. This was a very common strategy with men returning from the Second World War having seen and been through some extremely traumatic situations. Many have gone to their grave having never spoken of the terrible things they saw and experienced.

**Tasks:**

**1**. Take a legal pad and on the first line put the year you were born. On every other line list every year after that until now. In other words, allocate two lines for each calendar year.

**2.** Do your best to remember something that was emotionally significant for you for every calendar year you have listed. Anything at all, whether it was good or bad, painful or pleasurable, large or small. If you can think of more than one for each year that's great, but do try to find at least one for each year. You may have to consult with your family members or friends to help fill in some gaps — assuming they are still around.

**3.** Next to each event put a number between 0 and 10 that represents the degree of emotional stress it caused you, 10 being the highest.

**4.** Pay particular attention to any block of years during your childhood for which you draw a complete blank. It may mean that you have repressed the memory of something that may have been going on during that time. It's not always the case, but take a real good look at this if it applies to you. Ask for help in researching this period of time. However, be careful not to make wild assumptions or become suggestible to other people with an agenda who might plant ideas in your mind — about being abused for example. There have been many cases where therapists have done this, albeit unwittingly, but it has caused a great deal of needless pain and should be guarded against in your research.

**Warning:**
Don't be surprised if in doing this work you find yourself becoming unsettled or even quite upset. You may be stirring up some deeply buried unresolved material. So long as you are able to cope with it, this is good because it means that it is coming to the surface to be felt and then released. However, if you are mentally or emotionally unstable you would be wise to discontinue this work or do it only under the supervision of a trained psychotherapist, preferably one who has also trained as a Radical Forgiveness Coach. To find such a therapist, willing to work with you in person or by phone, go to our web site *www.radicalforgiveness.com.*

# Number Patterns

In the story, Steve Parker noticed that he had a pattern in his life where the number ten was significant. Situations would occur every ten years that were similar in terms of their emotional impact on him. This is quite common, so it might be interesting to do this for yourself.

**Tasks:**

1. Go back over your list of emotional events and see if you can notice one or more patterns emerging.

    Pattern 1: _____    weeks/months/years
    Pattern 2: _____    weeks/months/years
    Pattern 3: _____    weeks/months/years

2. Check whether a recurring number indicates the first wounding. For example, suppose you discover a pattern of nine. Check your list and ask yourself, what happened at age nine? What did I experience at that age that has tended to repeat itself over and over, albeit in thinly disguised ways, later in life? This could be the emotional event that led to a decision that might have run your life.

    At age _____ the following occurred: _____

    _____

    _____

    _____

    _____

    _____

continued .. /

_____

_____

_____

_____

_____

_____

As a result of that experience it is likely that I made a decision about life, or formed one or more beliefs about myself or other people that I carried through my life and played out in many situations. These are:

_____

_____

_____

_____

_____

_____

_____

_____

**Note:** As you are now aware, this was entirely purposeful because it leveraged the pain of the original wound. However, now that you have reached the point where this is no longer necessary, you should use the tools of Radical Forgiveness to free your mind from such decisions and to make new ones based on your current knowledge and understanding of who you are and what life is really about. (See Part Four.)

Research Assignment #6

# Relationship Questionnaire

Before analyzing the data you've just produced in Research Assignments 4 & 5, it is worth doing the following questionnaire. A similar version is available on the web site so you many have experienced it. Nevertheless, doing it here will help in your analysis of how you might have created your life experience from Day One — in particular how you might have used relationships as the means of feeling the pain of separation and accumulating a lot of karmic units.

**The Questionnaire**

**1. Reviewing your romantic relationships from high school on, look to see if any of the following applies to you:**

· My relationships all last roughly the same length of time before declining. **Y/N**
· My spouse has characteristics and behaviors similar to the parent of the same sex. **Y/N**
· I seem to attract the same kind of person to be in a relationship with each time. **Y/N**
· I seem unable to sustain a long term relationship. **Y/N**
· I always end up getting hurt. **Y/N**

If you answered **YES** to any of these questions, it means your soul has created an underlying energetic pattern that has been causing you to keep recreating these circumstances as the means of leveraging the pain of separation. That way you could create more karmic units more efficiently.

**Note:** Now that you have reached the Awakening phase, there is no need to continue doing this. Using the tools of Radical Forgiveness at this time will automatically dissolve the patterns and free you from the need to continue creating relationship dramas. (See Page 163.)

2. **Have any of the following repeatedly shown up in all your relationships?**

_ Betrayal
_ Abandonment
_ Severe disrespect
_ Being discounted and ignored
_ Lies and withholding of information
_ Control and manipulation
_ Cheating
_ Physical abuse
_ Emotional abuse
_ Severe rejection
_ Punishment
_ Other

If so, it is a reflection of a core-negative belief that you took on as a way to create many situations that reflected your need to be treated in this way. This, in turn, maximized your opportunity to feel this pain of separation so in that sense was an economical use of your energy. It gained you many karmic units for the least expenditure of energy.

**Note:** Now that you have reached the point where this is no longer necessary, you should use the tools of Radical Forgiveness to neutralize the core-negative belief so the behavior won't be repeated. (See Part Four.)

# Research Assignment #7

# Plot Your Journey

A t this point you should have a pretty good idea of all the situations and dramas that you created throughout the early part of your life in order to amass your 7,500 karmic units. Now let's plot your journey on the horizontal time line in order to see it graphically on the diagram you drew earlier on a large piece of paper, blackboard or whiteboard, like we did with Steve in the story. (It needs to be fairly big because it will finish up carrying a lot of detail.)

No need to take this too seriously, for it can only be approximate. But it's fun to do and you end up having it be a graphic representation not just of your life but your soul's journey too, at least up to the point of your Awakening.

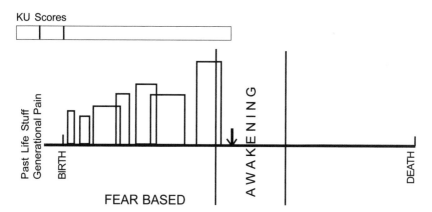

**Tasks:**

**1.** Bring forward your KU scores on past life bleedthrough and generational pain and put those in their respective boxes at the top.

**2.** From your initial list of events, take the most significant ones (let's say the ones you scored over 3), and place them in order on your time line. Some may have lasted longer than others and perhaps overlapped in time. Make an inspired guess at the number of karmic units each one of them earned you. Some things might have been more painful but lasted less time and vice versa. The total should add up to 7,500.

**3.** Beneath the line, indicate in block form how much pain you might have repressed, suppressed or projected onto others as a way of leveraging the pain.

Your graph will begin to look something like this:

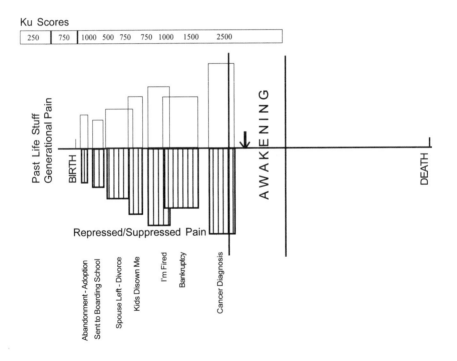

# Your Energy Expenditure

N ow that you have quantified your pain connected to the past in terms of the number of karmic units earned, it will be useful to bring it *down to earth* a bit to see if you can get some idea how much of your life force had to be expended to keep the stories in place. The idea of karmic units is an abstraction, but life force energy is real and very meaningful to all of us in a very practical way.

Caroline Myss in her book, *Why People Don't Heal and How They Can,* brought everyone's attention to this issue by showing that, even though Universal Energy is limitless, there is a limit to how much we can draw down and use at any one moment to power our lives. That means to be at our best, we have to optimize the use of that energy. But if it is being diverted to sustain our stories both past and future, we have precious little energy left for NOW.

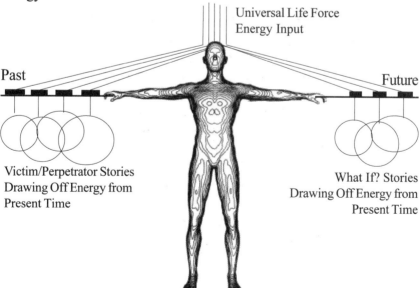

Universal Life Force
Energy Input

Past

Future

Victim/Perpetrator Stories
Drawing Off Energy from
Present Time

What If? Stories
Drawing Off Energy from
Present Time

87

It is very important to understand that our victim stories are very expensive on energy. And the deeper they are repressed or suppressed, the more energy it takes to keep them there. It's like when you try to push a beach ball under water. The more you push it down, the more strength it requires to keep it down. We also lose energy when we create *What If?* scenarios, constantly worrying about the future.

Caroline Myss was pointing out that if you have something like 70% of your energy invested in holding on to stories, both past and future, you don't have enough energy in present time to heal yourself. In that sense these stories can create ill-health and disease.

This is also very very important from a Radical Manifestation standpoint. Without your energy in present time to fuel your intentions, you are less likely to attract what you desire into your life.

**Tasks:**

**1. Victim/Perpetrator Stories:**
Go back to Research Assignment # 7 and for each story you scored karmic units relative to the pain felt at the time, make a subjective but honest assessment of how much of your life force energy it might still be taking NOW, to keep it running? Assume that you have 100 units of energy in total available to you at any one time.

(Remember, the more they were or are being suppressed, or even repressed, the more energy it takes to maintain them).

**Story #1:** Of the 100 units of energy I have available to me, I am still investing in this *victim/perpetrator* story approximately _____ units.

**Story #2:** Of the 100 units of energy I have available to me, I am still investing in this *victim/perpetrator* story approximately _____ units.

**Story #3:** Of the 100 units of energy I have available to me, I am still investing in this *victim/perpetrator* story approximately _____ units.

**Story #4:** Of the 100 units of energy I have available to me, I am still investing in this *victim/perpetrator* story approximately _____ units.

**Story #5:** Of the 100 units of energy I have available to me, I am still investing in this *victim/perpetrator* story approximately _____ units.

**Story #6:** Of the 100 units of energy I have available to me, I am still investing in this *victim/perpetrator* story approximately _____ units.

## 2. *What If?* Stories
I realize you haven't plotted your *What If?* stories, as such, yet but since they are energy suckers just like the other stories connected to the past, it makes sense to look at them now and assess now much energy is being leaked through them.

List the things you consistently worry about and create worst-case scenarios in your mind about how things might turn out.

**My *What If?* Stories:**

_____

_____

_____

_____

_____

_____

_____

_____

_____

89

*What If?* **Story #1:** Of the 100 units of energy I have available to me, I am still investing in this *What If?* story approximately _____ units.

*What If?* **Story #1:** Of the 100 units of energy I have available to me, I am still investing in this *What If?*story approximately _____ units.

*What If?* **Story #1:** Of the 100 units of energy I have available to me, I am still investing in this *What If?* story approximately _____ units.

*What If?* **Story #1:** Of the 100 units of energy I have available to me, I am still investing in this *What If?*story approximately _____ units.


**3. Total Up Your Energy Expenditure**
Add up all the scores in both *Victim/Perpetrator* and *What If?* stories. If it adds up to more than 100, you are dead! (You might want to go back and adjust some of your scores.) But be brutally honest with yourself.

"As I total all the units of energy I CURRENTLY have invested in my stories I realize that I only have _____ units of energy left for the NOW and I resolve to do whatever it takes to have retrieved most, if not all, of that energy within the shortest possible time."

**Note:** If your score is still relatively high, that's OK. You might expect it to be high. Remember, you needed the karmic units and you are only just beginning the Awakening Process. It's simply that you had to pay a high price in energy for those karmic units. But not to worry. As you awaken even more to the truth and begin doing the work in Part Three — the *Becoming Awake* Assignments, you will begin getting that energy back.

# Your Wake-Up Call

Y ou will have noticed that the diagram indicates that we experience progressively more pain as we go on. This is the way it normally works. Was it true for you?

Of course it is hard to compare the pain of a childhood wound with that experienced as an adult like, for instance, when a beloved spouse suddenly leaves. But what I think does hold true for most people is that the event that brings us to the point of Awakening is either the most painful experience of one's life, or the final straw in a long line of painful events. Either way, it brings us to a point of breakdown and ultimately, if bad enough, to the point where we surrender. In other words, it's our wake-up call or, as it sometimes called, our *dark night of the soul.*

In spiritual terms it means, of course, that we have reached our goal. We have gotten the number of karmic units we promised to accumulate during this lifetime. Therefore it's all perfect.

But, invariably, our Spiritual Intelligence makes sure that it's a *big one.* It has to be, otherwise it would not get our attention. It has to be big enough to shatter our current world view, undermine everything that we have ever held to be self-evidently true and immutable. It has to be powerful enough to at least begin the process of busting apart our victim stories. It has to shake the very foundations of our life and our beliefs about who we are and our purpose for being here.

Now, I have no way of knowing whether you are in the middle of this crisis, just emerging from the experience or looking back at it now with the benefit of 20/20 hindsight. But wherever you are with this, you need to recognize its importance. You need to honor yourself for having the courage to go through it for the sake of your soul's growth. I'm sure Harley would have warned you ahead of time that what looks incredibly easy from up there can be extremely difficult once you are in a human body — a body that is capable of such intense feeling. You have truly earned your karmic units.

**Tasks:**

**1.** If you are looking back at this experience having processed it out completely and have no more pain attached to it, then it would still be a good idea to write about it in terms that connect it to the myth we are creating here. That is, far from doing anything TO you, they did it all FOR you and the whole thing was perfect in that sense.

If you didn't work through it using the Radical Forgiveness tools, I would definitely recommend that you go back over it and do as many Radical Forgiveness Worksheets as necessary to make sure that all the energy around it is released and that all you feel for those who were *responsible* for your pain is love and gratitude.

I don't suggest you write more than a paragraph or two here because your story is very likely to be extremely personal and you wouldn't want others to read it. Better that you write it somewhere else or on your own computer so you can keep it private.

**2.** If you are only just emerging from, or are still in the midst of the experience and still feeling the pain of it, I have two pieces of advice for you:

    a) Give yourself total permission to feel all the pain — don't do a *spiritual bypass*.

Doing a *spiritual bypass* means suppressing the feelings by going too quickly to a spiritual interpretation of the event. This ranges from making excuses for the person out of compassion and understanding, to immediately *seeing the spiritual perfection in the situation.*

Remember, the whole point of creating the situation in the first place is to have the feeling experience. Any time you use a method that stops the flow of feelings, you are getting in your own way. The feelings must be felt first. Only then can you shift into Radical Forgiveness.

> b) Avail yourself of some Radical Forgiveness Coaching and do a lot of Radical Forgiveness Worksheets until the pain stops and you can feel gratitude for what happened.

It is hard to do this alone. A Radical Forgiveness Coach can give you a tremendous amount of support in both feeling the feelings and helping you move into Radical Forgiveness. This is particularly helpful if you are afraid to let yourself feel your feelings fully. Even having a friend with you who would be willing to support you non-judgmentally in expressing your feelings openly while you tell your story would be helpful.

If you feel able to do it, I would suggest you now tell a brief version of your story here on this and the next page, just to get it down, but as I suggest above, write the more private parts of the story in some other place more secure.

**My Wake-Up Call:** _____

_____

_____

_____

_____

_____

_____

_____

...continued/

Research Assignment #10

# After the Awakening

Having reviewed all that brought you to the point of Awakening, (my having made the assumption that you wouldn't be reading this book if you were not yet there), the next thing is to ask yourself what might come after the Awakening?

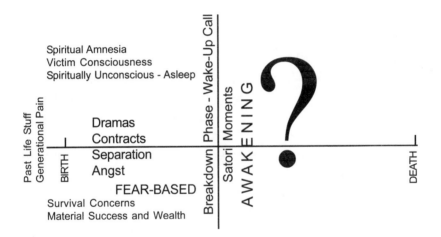

Now, as I said before, I don't know whether you are still only just coming into the Awakening phase, or you have already put a lot of life experience between that and the present. However, for the sake of clarity, I am going to assume that I am addressing readers who have recently emerged from the breakdown phase. That is to say, they are no longer hurting to the extent that they cannot move on with their lives and begin to grow from the experience. I am also going to assume that they have had a few Satori experiences that have caused them to heed the call to open their minds to the metaphysical paradigm of reality. (See Page 157.) They will have shifted their consciousness to the extent that they are committed to taking responsibility for their own lives, shifting out of victim consciousness and opening their hearts to their fellow human beings.

I say this because I believe this is what it means to have an Awakening. I base this on what I have observed in more than a decade of taking people through the breakdown experience into an Awakening during what I call **The Miracles** workshop. This has nothing to do with *A Course in Miracles,*\* I hasten to add, but has everything to do with the fact that miracles literally do occur as a result of the people going through the experience and waking up to the truth.

By way of contrast, let me repeat what I said earlier about how we (necessarily) think, act and feel during the period of our lives before the Awakening. I said that during that phase we are spiritually unconscious and unaware of spiritual reality beyond the superficial or institutional. We tend to be focused on the world *out there* rather than the world *in here*. We are concerned with survival, making money, creating material success, accumulating wealth, controlling as many aspects of life as possible and seeing life as a zero sum game. In short we are committed to victim consciousness and acting from a world view that supports a fear based way of thinking.

People who come through this process of Awakening also tend to change their values quite considerably. They develop an understanding of the Law of Karma (what goes around, comes around), so they become much more committed to living in integrity and operating on the basis of honesty and fairness. They become much less hard-nosed, and much more heart centered in how they deal with people.

Whereas before they were primarily concerned with creating money, a lavish lifestyle, material success and wealth for themselves and their

---

*A Course in Miracles, Published in 1975 by the Foundation for Inner Peace and since 1996 by The Foundation for ACIM.

families, they have become much more concerned with community, being of service and making a difference in the world. Their fulfillment is typically in promoting social justice, protecting the environment and doing work that is satisfying and meaningful. This is why a lot of people in this phase of life are wanting to change careers — most often from one that is rooted in the old value system to one where they feel that can make a difference in other people's lives, even if it means less money and prestige.

However, this is not to say that they don't continue experiencing drama in their lives, just the same as before. Of course they do, because life goes on. They continue to interact with other human beings in the classroom of life and continue to engage in the required curriculum.

The big difference, though, is that they begin to participate with awareness. Instead of being unconscious as before, they are now aware. They have developed what we call the *Observer.* This is a part of us that has the ability to witness ourselves being ourselves. It is said that we are the only creatures able to do this, but I have my doubts about that. How do we know that an ant is not self-aware?

Another distinction between how one is after the Awakening compared to before is that the Awakened person becomes able to move through an upset very quickly. Whereas someone with a victim consciousness might stay in anger and resentment for months, if not years , an Awakened person can certainly have strong feelings about something, but he or she is able to allow the emotions to flow through and out very quickly. (English literature is full of dramatic tales about family feuds that went on for generations.) There are two reasons for this:

1) The Observer watches. It sees us getting angry but does not judge. It loves us in our anger — for there is purpose and meaning in it. But once the emotion has been felt and expressed, and any necessary action taken, then the purpose has been served. It nudges us to let the emotion flow out. Since an emotion is a thought attached to a feeling, our Observer reminds us to release the thought (which is seldom true)

97

and simply feel the feeling. After a moment or two, the feeling naturally subsides.

2) When you know the truth — that at the spiritual level there is nothing wrong or bad happening, it doesn't take long before that knowingness comes to the surface and cools the emotions, no matter what they are. How can you stay mad at someone you know deep down is a soul who agreed to lovingly dance with you in this way?

Not only does the Awakened person move through his or her feelings quickly when upsets occur, but as time goes on and the Awakening really takes hold, situations actually cease to become the upsets they would have been in earlier times. A truly Awakened person is able to stay completely calm, alert and peaceful even in the most upsetting of circumstances.

Let's see how this might look now on the diagram.

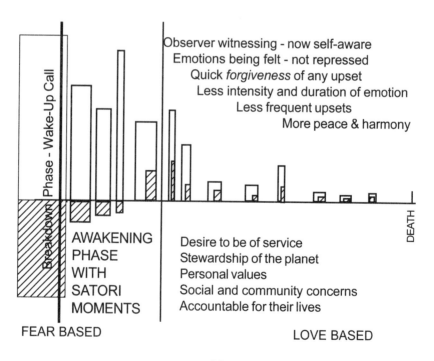

Observer witnessing - now self-aware
Emotions being felt - not repressed
Quick *forgiveness* of any upset
Less intensity and duration of emotion
Less frequent upsets
More peace & harmony

Breakdown Phase - Wake-Up Call

AWAKENING PHASE WITH SATORI MOMENTS

DEATH

Desire to be of service
Stewardship of the planet
Personal values
Social and community concerns
Accountable for their lives

FEAR BASED

LOVE BASED

What to notice about the foregoing diagram is:

a) that the breakdown phase actually becomes part of the Awakening phase and precipitates the transformation,

b) that dramas continue to occur during the Awakening phase but decrease in frequency, duration and intensity of emotion as time goes on,

c) that whereas prior to the Awakening most feelings around the dramas were either denied, repressed or projected onto others, (represented by being below the line), the person becomes more and more present to and willing to own their feelings as soon as they arise (represented by being above the line).

d) that the life experience is shifting from a predominantly fear-based vibration to a love-based vibration as we begin to remember that we truly are Love.

What is not self-evident from all of the foregoing, is the effect that this has on the collective consciousness of the whole human race. When someone goes through their Awakening, it has the effect of not only raising their own vibration but of raising the consciousness of the planet.

Anyway, we are now at the point where the two halves of the diagram depicting the entire time line of a soul's journey in a human body can come together. I realize of course, that you have not completed your own yet because you are not actually dead but if your review chart were complete this is how it might look.

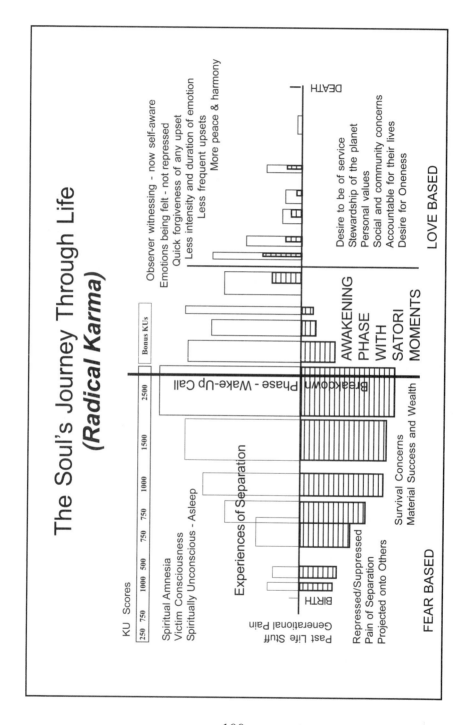

100

# Putting it All Together

In order to complete the diagram you began in Research Assignment #7, in which you plotted everything up to the point of breakdown and the Awakening, I suggest you now plot what has happened since then. If it is the case that you are only just a few days or weeks away from that moment then there isn't much you can add, obviously. On the other hand, if some significant time has passed between now and the first Satori, then you will inevitably have some things to plot and your diagram will end up looking something like the one on the previous page.

When you plot what has occurred since the Awakening, take into account what was said in the previous chapter and see whether the generalities stated there applied in your case. Be as accurate as you can and be honest with yourself. Remember, this is not about judging your *spiritual correctness* or your *degree of enlightenment*, for there is no such thing. To believe in degrees of enlightenment is to believe in spiritual elitism and I am against that. My belief is that no one is any further along on their spiritual path than anyone else.

Nevertheless, this part of the exercise is perhaps more important than the earlier part in that it will become a guide for how you might live out the rest of your incarnation as an awake human being. If, as I suggested in Research Assignment #8, you wrote about your wake-up call in your journal, I would add a new suggestion that you augment the diagram by writing about how your life has changed since then. Write about what you have observed about yourself and learned about life that is different from before the Awakening. You can also express how you are going to take what you have learned into the future. If you wish to write more than the space allows here, continue writing in your journal.

**How My Life Has Changed Since My Awakening:**

# Preface to Part Three

# Clean Up, Consolidate and Stay Awake

I t is not uncommon for people to come through to a genuine Awakening after a breakdown experience, and then within a few months go right back to sleep again. The experience may have been too demanding for them. It may have stripped away too much that was normal and comfortable and undermined everything in which they felt secure.

It may also have been the case that the breakdown came a little too early or was not completed. They might simply have needed more time in Victimland. Whatever the reason, it is perfect.

Having said that, the truth is that Victimland is a seductive place and it's very easy for any of us to be pulled back there. We do have the tools to help us emerge if we go there temporarily, but in addressing you as someone who is newly emerged from breakdown and into the initial phase of the Awakening, (as I do all my readers so we can work this together, no matter where you are on the time line), I need to ask whether you are fully committed to staying Awake.

If so, then this part of the book will help you do that. It will help you consolidate your new vibrational pattern and progressively raise your vibration as you move into the future. It will help you go deeper into the Awakening experience so you become more empowered to make a difference in the world. This is because as you increase your spiritual energy you will be operating more from *love* than *fear*. You will be more trusting, more surrendered and more open to what needs to happen.

It is clear to me that the post-Awakening period is every bit as demanding as the pre-Awakening period, but in a very different way. Whereas the first half was about living in denial, shirking personal responsibility by blaming everything on everyone else and being a victim, the second half demands that we be self-accountable, honest, humble, open and always in integrity.

Obviously, this doesn't happen overnight. In fact it takes a commitment to continuing growth and development until the end of one's life. However, in order to begin the process of transformation there are some things you must do in the next weeks, months and even years in order to consolidate the Awakening and make it a part of who you are. These are listed as *Growth Assignments* in the pages that follow.

There are other things in Part Three that are not so much assignments as recommendations. I hope you will give them due considerations.

# PART THREE

Becoming Awake
and
Staying Awake

# Clean Up the Past

Using the knowledge that you have acquired from this book and/or my book entitled *Radical Forgiveness, Making Room for the Miracle,* make a return journey along the time line you have just drawn and complete as many **Radical Forgiveness Worksheets** as it takes to dissolve the energy attached to each and every one of those events or situations. You may already have done a lot of this work in Research Assignment # 4 — Your Emotional History. Nevertheless, go right back to your birth and don't leave out even one story.

In addition to working on those that you have put on your time line, look over the initial list you made as part of Research Assignment # 4 to see if there are any situations that might need some work done on them to clear the energy. Make a forgiveness list on the next page.

(See *Part Four: The Tools of Radical Forgiveness* for details of how to use the downloadable Radical Forgiveness Worksheet.)

This work is going to take some time and some effort. Spread it out over a number of weeks/months and make sure you do as many worksheets as is necessary to get you to the point where there is no charge left on that situation. (It might take a lot of worksheets to get there in some cases.) If you end up feeling gratitude for what happened so much the better.

To augment the worksheets, use the **13 Steps Radical Forgiveness process on the CD** as often as you can. It takes less time to do it and you can keep it in your car. (See Page 183.)

# A Forgiveness List

I resolve to do Radical Forgiveness Worksheets on the following:

_____     _____
_____     _____
_____     _____
_____     _____
_____     _____
_____     _____
_____     _____
_____     _____
_____     _____
_____     _____
_____     _____
_____     _____
_____     _____
_____     _____
_____     _____
_____     _____
_____     _____
_____     _____
_____     _____
_____     _____
_____     _____
_____     _____
_____     _____

# Forgive Yourself

It is vital that you work on forgiving yourself for I know full well that you are full of guilt, shame and self recrimination for all the bad things you think you have done and have, at times, become. It is a byproduct of the life you have led up to the Awakening. Victim consciousness needed perpetrators as much as it needed victims, and there were times when you were called to be a victim and there were times when you were a perpetrator. That's just how it was. But it created a lot of guilt and shame and it has to be released now if you are to go forward.

Most people find it harder to forgive themselves than to forgive others, even when they have come to see that there is nothing to forgive anyone for. I imagine that you are no different in this respect. I also imagine that you are your own worst critic when it comes to looking at who and what you are. That internal judge doesn't just stop when you awaken. You have to work to silence it.

This why I have developed two very powerful **online programs** that apply the same Radical Forgiveness philosophy to both self-forgiveness and self-acceptance. The former neutralizes the guilt while the latter takes away the shame.

Nothing will be more likely to seduce you into falling back to sleep than unresolved, unconscious self-hatred, which is why I urge you to enroll in these programs in order to clean up that part of your psyche as soon as possible. It includes a bonus program to help you release toxic secrets. (For details, see the Appendix, Page 196.)

# My Self-Hatred Inventory

Things I haven't forgiven myself for or accepted in myself:

_____

_____

_____

_____

_____

_____

_____

_____

_____

_____

_____

_____

_____

_____

_____

_____

_____

_____

_____

_____

_____

_____

_____

_____

_____

_____

_____

_____

# Halt Generational Pain

The task here is to make every effort to heal any generational pain you have in you and to stop passing it on to your children and grandchildren. This is extremely important for you, for future generations and for the collective consciousness.

If you took it from an individual, give it back. If you are carrying it for your ancestors or your race, drop it. You have no right to carry it on and you are doing nothing but harm. Remember and honor your ancestor's suffering and their courage to survive it but give it no more energy than that. What right do you have to say they should never have had the experience when you know now that it was chosen? You can only respect their soul's choice.

Refuse to listen to or continue buying into other people's old victim stories, especially family stories and secrets. That may lose you some points and some friends, but so be it. It has to stop or it will stop you. And refuse to pass them on to your children.

The best way to release generational pain is to first do the forgiveness work using the tools of Radical Forgiveness. Forgive everyone involved, including any individuals, groups, armies, governments, leaders, politicians, religious leaders, God, etc.

Then create a ceremony in which there is a ritual transmutation of the pain and a letting go. Use fire in the ceremony if possible. Collapse the energy field by affirming that what happened back then was perfect in the spiritual sense and that God does not make mistakes.

## My  Inventory of Generational Pain

Things I am angry or sad about that had nothing to do with me but which I took on as my own, have held ever since and now recognize I have no right to hold:

_____

_____

_____

_____

_____

_____

_____

_____

_____

_____

_____

_____

_____

_____

_____

_____

_____

_____

_____

_____

_____

_____

_____

*I give them back and let them go!*

# Heal Past Lives

If you identified some past life bleedthrough in your life review, and you have determined that it is still active in your life, then this is the moment to take action to process it through and OUT. If it is manifesting as a phobia or something of that nature, get some help from a good hypnotherapist who knows how to treat phobias.

However, the most important thing for you to do now is to invoke the power of your Spiritual Intelligence (or your Higher Self) to break the connection between this life and the old one so long as it is in your highest and best interest to do so. And take no part in making that assessment. Your Ego is in no way equipped to make that call. Simply affirm that any and all past life agreements and contracts are complete, cancelled or already null and void unless, that is, your Spiritual Intelligence decides otherwise. And leave it at that. I suggest that you avoid *past life readers* from now on.

**Notes on Past Lives:** _____

_____

_____

_____

_____

_____

_____

_____

_____

_____

.../continued

# Grieve Your Losses

W e have found that unresolved grief is the principle cause of pain in many people. It is a very toxic energy and it needs to be felt and released in a healthy manner.

Compared to others around the world, people in the West are not good at grieving. Instead of expressing it outwardly and vocally through screaming and wailing and physically through flailing, stamping and whirling, as they do in the Middle East for example, people in the West process it inwardly, stoically, silently and, in England anyway, with stiff upper lips. Grief festers in them and frequently it turns to anger, rage and depression. In many cases it comes out as a physical disease like cancer. When you ask a cancer patient what happened to them five to seven years before the onset of cancer, they will nearly always tell you about a severe loss. That's how toxic it is!

It is vitally important therefore that you give yourself permission to feel any grief that remains yet to be felt and to release any thoughts and beliefs that are attached to those feelings. (An emotion is a thought attached to a feeling.) When you have discovered the thoughts and beliefs connected to the grief, do the forgiveness work around anyone implicated in the situation and then reframe your beliefs.

For example, when someone dies in what seems to be a tragic and untimely way you are bound to feel the grief around the loss — your loss, that is. But it's your belief that it was tragic, untimely and something to seek revenge for that turns your grief into suffering. The reframe is that it is not tragic for the person who died because they are now where they wanted to be. And that's because death is a choice — and it's not even death.

# My Inventory of Losses

Things I have had taken away from me and for which I might still have some residual grief residing in me:

| LOSSES | BELIEFS TO REFRAME |
| --- | --- |
|  |  |
|  |  |
|  |  |
|  |  |
|  |  |
|  |  |
|  |  |
|  |  |
|  |  |
|  |  |
|  |  |
|  |  |
|  |  |
|  |  |
|  |  |
|  |  |
|  |  |
|  |  |
|  |  |
|  |  |

I am committed to feeling the grief and reframing the beliefs I have around the loss.

# Release Judgment & Expectation

It's simply part of being human to have plenty of judgments and expectations. It is what humans do. But once we have reached the point of Awakening, it is demanded of us that we learn how to handle these aspects of the human personality so that we judge less and at least modify our need for others and the world to meet our expectations. That way we avoid disempowerment, suffer less disappointment and maintain a high vibration.

One of the most important items on the Radical Forgiveness worksheet (See Page 165), is the following:

*"My discomfort is/was my signal that I am/was withholding love from myself and _____ by judging, holding expectations, wanting _____ to change and seeing _____ as less than perfect."*

Radical Forgiveness teaches us that in terms of the spiritual big picture, everyone is playing their part in the Divine Plan exactly as they should. Who are we to demand that they be different? Our need to have people be different to the way they are is fear based.

This is not to say that we allow people to abuse us or mistreat us. If someone is toxic and does not respond to your acceptance of them just the way they are, then drop the relationship. Accept them the way they are and move on.

Also, look to see what part of them or their behavior is a mirror for you. It may be that your judgment of the person is a reflection of what you judge in yourself. IF YOU SPOT IT - YOU GOT IT!

## My Judgments and Expectations

I am noticing that I have a lot of outstanding judgments and expectations against the following and recognize that I am seeing in them what I am not willing to love and accept in myself:

PERSON                              JUDGMENT/EXPECTATION

_____    _____

_____    _____

_____    _____

_____    _____

_____    _____

_____    _____

_____    _____

_____    _____

_____    _____

_____    _____

_____    _____

_____    _____

_____    _____

_____    _____

_____    _____

_____    _____

I totally release my need for these people to be different and free them to be who they are without judgment and I hereby declare myself free to interact with them or not. I am free to do what is best for me and I am responsible only for myself.

# Fake It Till You Make It

By this I mean forming the habit of always thinking, reacting and behaving as if you firmly believed in the Radical Forgiveness philosophy. Yes, I did say, "AS IF." Let me explain.

Right at the beginning of this book I said that belief wasn't necessary. Radical Forgiveness is a spiritual process, not an intellectual one. It invokes our Spiritual Intelligence and works at the highest level of operation about which we know little. We simply don't yet know the mind of God. But it's enough to know that Radical Forgiveness works.

Having said all that, the way to make it a habit is to regularly use the tools that the Radical Forgiveness technology provides, not only to clean up the past, but to deal with every little irritation and annoyance that come your way on a daily basis. And there will be plenty of them, I promise you, because when you commit to the Awakening process, Spirit gives you plenty of opportunity to test your commitment. If you think the early days of the Awakening are a walk in the park, you may be in for a shock. You will need every bit of help you can get. **The tools you might make use of are:**

> The Radical Forgiveness Worksheet (free — downloadable)
> The Free Online Radical Forgiveness Worksheet Program
> The 13 Steps to Radical Forgiveness CD
> The 13 Steps to Radical Self-Forgiveness/Self Acceptance CD
> The 7 Step Process for Radical Forgiveness CD
> The 4 Steps to Radical Forgiveness Process
> The Multimedia Radical Empowerment Program

(For the details on each of these see Part 4 and the Appendix.)

## Other Things You Might Do

**1. Take the Radical Empowerment Program.**  This is a 12-month, multi-media learning program that extends the technology of Radical Forgiveness into that of Radical Manifestation, the art of conscious creating.  Whereas Radical Forgiveness is for cleaning up the past, Radical Manifestation is about creating the future. Put the two together and you get Radical Empowerment.

$$RF + RM = RE$$

This program will take you well beyond the early Awakening stage in the 12 month period — assuming you follow the program, of course. It is designed to get Radical Forgiveness so deeply anchored into your body and mind that it becomes your natural way of being — your default way of acting, thinking and behaving.  You will find detailed information at *www.radicalempowerment.com.*

**2. Hire an RF Coach.**  There are trained Radical Forgiveness Coaches available to help you gain competence in the use of the tools and to assist you with the issues that challenge you most. Should you wish to take advantage of this service, you will find them listed geographically on our web site, but since most of it is done on the phone, it really doesn't matter where they live. Pick whoever feels right and give him or her a call.

**3. Take a Workshop**. This is an option which will put you on the fast track.  These vary in length and depth, but you can read about the various programs we offer on our web site, which is *www.radicalforgiveness.com.*  I can assure you that by the time you have done either of the main workshops you will have cleared out most if not all of your stories and cleaned up much of your past.

*[I am sorry if some of this sounds like marketing.  But if I am to give you this valuable information regarding tools that will help you continue your Awakening, I have no choice since not all of them are free.  I make as much as I can available at no charge, but obviously I must charge for some things.]*

# Discover Your Purpose

I pointed out earlier that a high proportion of people who go through the Awakening have decided that they want to change careers. What they have done as a career in the past has been rooted in a world and a way of relating to other people and the environment they no longer identify with or wish to support. Their values have changed and in order to be in integrity they find themselves wanting to contribute in alignment with those values.

A Buddhist monk known to a friend of mine, Darryl Dennis, said something that changed Darryl's life and gave her her life's mission. He said: *"Every person must be given the opportunity to contribute a part of him/herself to something bigger than him/herself at least once during his or her lifetime. If not they will feel that their life has been without meaning or purpose."*

Some people have clarity about their purpose while others have very little idea of what that might be. They just know that they want to do something that will give them fulfillment, satisfaction, joy, and a knowing that what they do is of service and value to others. Many of them have had very little experience in such fields and it is not uncommon for them to have unrealistic expectations. After all, not everyone can become a massage therapist.

Money also seems to be a major factor for many, especially for those who still have to earn a living at what they do. However, the truth is that there's no shortage of money, so it really should not be a block. It is only old paradigm thinking that makes it so.

What does matter, though, is the mission and purpose they came in to fulfill. When they align with that, everything works. They become totally supported and fully supplied with money and other resources.

Before going any further, let's make a distinction between mission and purpose. They are very similar and at times may mean the same but for clarity we should separate them.

**a) Mission.** This is a specific thing that we agreed prior to incarnating. For example, my mission is *"to raise the consciousness of the planet through Radical Forgiveness and to create a world of forgiveness by 2012."*

**b) Purpose.** This is what we do here on planet Earth that supports the mission. Again, using my own example, *"my purpose is to use my writing and speaking skills to bring the concept of Radical Forgiveness to as many people as I can and to train others to do the same."*

The mission is grandiose and visionary while purpose is more grounded in creative action and forward movement. Basically, the purpose supports the mission. It is seldom that you know your mission before you have become connected with your purpose.

There's a reason why you may not know your purpose. One of the things you agreed to be afflicted with when you incarnated was spiritual amnesia. It was necessary that you forgot all about your prior arrangements so you would play the game for real. But, along with everything else, you forgot your mission. It would be something that you would discover when you Awakened.

For example, you might find yourself being led to do something or go somewhere for no real reason other than it feels right. That would be your Spiritual Intelligence moving you towards your purpose. You would know when you had found it when you felt infused with joy, passion and fulfillment in what you do with your life. It need not be in how you make your primary living. It could be your hobby or some other activity that juices you in this way.

## Tasks:

1. If you know it, give a description of what you feel is your life purpose. Is there a specific mission associated with it? Does it translate into a possible career for you? If so what kind of career? Are you doing it now, or do you plan to transition into it — if so when?

_____

_____

_____

_____

_____

_____

_____

_____

_____

_____

_____

_____

_____

_____

**2.** If you don't know what your purpose is or you have not got it clarified to the degree you would like, use the following procedure to tease out what it might be.

Before you begin this process, though, and in case you are worried about not knowing what your purpose is, let me put this in perspective for you by making the following point: There is no one who is without a purpose for being here. ***Just being here IS our purpose.*** That's precisely why we came here. So don't worry if you have not found a more specific, concrete purpose yet. Perhaps there isn't anything else. If not, that's OK.

That said, however, it is likely that your journey will involve other specific intentions of a spiritual nature that you have agreed to take on either before incarnating or as you go along. And, as we have already said, they are usually oriented towards serving others in some profound and meaningful way and can involve the sharing of one's particular gifts and talents.

So let's start there. *(The following procedure appears in Chapter 22 of my book, Radical Manifestation, The Fine Art of Creating the Life You Want.)*

## Step One — Your Gifts & Talents

Make a list of all your talents, skills, capabilities, interests and personal qualities that you are aware of.

> *Example:*
>
> | | |
> |---|---|
> | *Creative* | *Good dancer* |
> | *Artistic (painter)* | *Good leader* |
> | *Patient* | *Friendly* |
> | *Good researcher* | *Compassionate* |
> | *Good with people* | *Teaching ability* |
> | *Good with children* | *Academic* |
> | *Good speaker* | *Musicianship* |

## Add In What Others Might See in You

Ask some people close to you — friends, family, colleagues, etc., what skills, talents, qualities and capabilities they see in you and appreciate about you. Add to your list those you had not already seen in yourself.

## Rate Your Level of Proficiency in Each

Rate each talent or skill on a scale of 0-100 according to the level of proficiency you have in each one on the list. Zero is none whatsoever, while 100 would be total mastery. 50 would be average proficiency. Be as objective as you can about this. Ask others if necessary.

*Example:*

| | | | |
|---|---|---|---|
| *Creative* | *70* | *Good dancer* | *20* |
| *Artistic (painter)* | *40* | *Good leader* | *50* |
| *Patient* | *--* | *Friendly* | *--* |
| *Good researcher* | *40* | *Compassionate* | *--* |
| *Good with people* | *--* | *Teaching ability* | *60* |
| *Good with children* | *--* | *Academic* | *40* |
| *Good speaker* | *30* | *Musicianship* | *60* |

## Assess Your Passion For Each

Rate each one on a scale of 0-100 according to how much **passion** you have for expressing each one of the items on the list. Zero would mean you hate doing it and would never do it by choice. 100 would mean that it gives you total joy and you resent every moment that you are not doing it. 50 would mean that you don't feel strongly either way. In other words you quite enjoy doing it when you are, but wouldn't necessarily go out of your way to do it. Be careful not to score them on the basis of how much approval it gets you. That might feel good but it is secondary to the feeling that arises simply out of doing it. One way to check this is to note how you feel in your gut when you say the word or think about expressing that quality or talent. Is it positive or negative? Does is make you feel good, or not?

*Example:*

|  | *Proficiency* | *Passion* |
|---|---|---|
| *Creative* | 70 | 80 |
| *Artistic (painter)* | 40 | 95 |
| *Patience* | -- | 60 |
| *Good researcher* | 40 | 5 |
| *Good with people* | -- | 20 |
| *Good with children* | -- | 60 |
| *Good speaker* | 30 | 10 |
| *Musicianship* | 60 | 70 |
| *Academic* | 40 | 10 |
| *Dance* | 20 | 40 |
| *Good leader* | 20 | 20 |
| *Friendly* | -- | 50 |
| *Compassion* | -- | 60 |
| *Teaching ability* | 60 | 70 |

**Note:** Proficiency does not necessarily equate with passion or even enjoyment. The person in the example above is good academically and good at research, but enjoys neither. His/her painting skill is the same as those two and not great, but he or she shows enormous passion for the activity.

## Step Two — How You Love to Express Them

Select up to five items that score high on the passion scale, irrespective of how much proficiency you have in each one, and then write down how you like to express them.

Example:

### a) Creativity:

*I like to express my creativity by exploring new ways of seeing things and expressing my perceptions visually through painting in all sorts of different media, dance and music.*

### b) Painting:

*I love to lose myself in the painting process and in expressing my feelings that way, learn about myself and the world around me because I see everything in new and exciting ways.*

### c) Musicianship:

*I love to play the piano and keyboard instruments and to experiment with sounds and harmonies that I can relate to my painting in a multi-media format.*

### d) Teaching ability:

*I love working with children because they are so creative and free when allowed to be so. I seem to be able to bring that out in them.*

## Step Three — My Purpose Is . . .

Pulling it all together now, create a grandiose purpose statement of what you would be achieving or doing if you were expressing all these talents in the way that would be totally enjoyable to you and where there are no limits on you.

*Example:*

*My purpose is to use my compassion, my patience, and my ability to inspire children in awakening and nurturing their creative spirit through expressing my passion for artistic endeavor through painting, dance and music as a demonstration to them of the power of the arts to bring joy to millions of people.*

### Simplify

Now edit it down to a short memorable statement. The above statement covers all the bases, but it is long and cumbersome. It would be hard to remember. A purpose statement needs to be something you repeat often, so it should be short, easy to say and easily memorized.

129

*Example:*

> *My purpose is to inspire all children to free their creative spirit and to find joy in the creative process, while I, too, soar in my own creative power as an artist.*

## How Does it Feel?

Check to see if you have it right, by registering how it feels to you. Keep massaging it until it feels good, like it really fits. If it doesn't feel wonderful, look again to see if you have put the wrong thing first. For instance, in this example, the lists show that the real juice was in being the artist, especially painting, which he or she scored at "95". Children and teaching came in at "60" and "70," respectively. I would want to ask whether this person was actually selling out by going for what seemed possible or achievable rather than what was really in his or her heart?

Let's try it again. Here's another version where the painting becomes the primary purpose and the teaching of children secondary:

> *My purpose is to change the way that millions of people see the world by using my skill as a painter, musician and dancer to bring them to a new understanding of reality and employ my teaching ability to open the hearts and minds of children to the joy in the creative process.*

And then, edited down:

> *My purpose is to change the world through my art by opening people's eyes to what is meaningful while freeing the creative spirit in children.*

This seems more in alignment with the real purpose. It doesn't matter that the proficiency is not yet very high. That can be attained through training. Getting the training is exactly the thing this person can use the *Radical Manifestation* technology to create. With that much intention (95 percent passion), it is virtually guaranteed!

## Memorize It

Once you have a purpose statement, commit it to memory and let it be your touchstone in relation to everything that you do. If you have a difficult decision to make, ask yourself which option is most aligned with your purpose statement. The more aligned you stay with your purpose the more powerful you will be and the more you will be able to manifest what you want in your life.

## Keep Checking It

If it doesn't feel quite right for you, massage it some more until it does feel right. You might find that it will suit you for some months or even years, but then might need to be modified in response to a shift in your own priorities and preferences. You'll know.

## Enroll Others

The moment you get someone else even a little bit excited about your mission or purpose, you will have magnified the energy of it many times over. But choose very carefully who to share it with and how. To tell it to someone who is likely to have little understanding or resonance with it is to invite some negativity and that could suck the energy right out of it. Choose carefully and you will get the support you need to live your purpose. In 'Becoming Awake' Assignment #10, I am going to try to enroll you in mine.

# Create Consciously

It was all part of victim consciousness to believe that what turned up in your life was simply a matter of chance or, (if you tended to invoke superstition rather than statistical probability), luck. We are increasingly becoming aware — as part of the Awakening process — that there is nothing random about it at all. What shows up *out there* is a projection of what's *in here*. Simply put, we create our reality by our thoughts, beliefs and intentions, and we empower them through our emotions. The creative force in the world is consciousness.

Coming to this realization is part of what it means to awaken. Looking back of course, you will see evidence of it in your own life and in the life of the collective. In doing your life review, you realized that you created circumstances in your life that served your purpose wonderfully in helping you accumulate your karmic units. There was no luck or chance involved in any of that. You got exactly what you wanted. It was, and is still, the same for the oversoul of the collective. The whole human race is creating exactly what it wants for its own growth and spiritual evolution.

In that phase of your journey, you were doing it unconsciously and specifically for the purpose of creating experiences of separation. But now you have Awakened and you have the luxury of creating with full awareness. You can choose what to create, or what not to create, and be conscious of the reasons why.

This seems like a blessing, and it really is one. But it is also a responsibility. Your conscious choices carry a very different vibration to those that served your (highest) purpose when you were unconscious. If you use your creative energy now, as an Awakened person, to manifest things that harm the environment, degrade human dignity or hurt others in any way, your own vibration will go down and you will be contributing to a corresponding decrease in the vibration of the planet as a whole. As an Awakened person, I'm sure you would want your vibration to keep on going up and your contribution to the planetary vibration to be positive.

However, I do not wish to imply that you should not manifest things of a material nature or that are just *nice to have*. But it is a question of how best to use your creative energies. In my book, *Radical Manifestation, The Fine Art of Creating the Life You Want,* I refer to the following three levels of intention. Use these to think through the question of energy usage for yourself so you achieve a balance consistent with your values and your purpose.

1. **Baseline Intentions:** These relate to our simple desires to manifest things, conditions or situations that we feel will benefit us in terms of our physical and emotional well being. Included in this category would be an adequate supply of money, a comfortable home, a good job or profitable business, a certain type of car, a satisfying relationship and so on.

2. **Transformational Intentions:** These relate more to our desire for self-improvement and personal growth. They would include the right educational program, the perfect life coach, the most satisfying and meaningful career opportunity, etc.

3. **Transpersonal Intentions:** These relate to our desires to create for reasons that are beyond self. The motivation is to do good for others, for the collective and for the environment, etc. They might include ending hunger around the world, finding a cure for AIDS, envisioning peace in the Middle East, ending female genital mutilation, child abuse and other issues of social justice and humanitarian concerns.

Ideally each level should reference the one above it. In other words, when you give a reason why you wish to manifest at the baseline level, it will have more meaning, a higher vibration and therefore more power if it is linked to a desire emanating from one or both of the levels above the baseline. Having said that, though, if it is a baseline intention only and it is something you want and feel you deserve, go for it!

Let me give you what I think is the best description of how the manifestation process actually works and what we mean when we say that there is no shortage of anything and that it is a totally abundant universe. It comes from the work of physicist David Bohm.

Bohm says that the reality of everyday life is simply an illusion, just like a holographic image. Beneath the so called objective reality lies a deeper order of reality that continually gives birth to the material world.

He called this level of reality the *implicate order* in which things that are not yet manifest are **en***folded*, just waiting to be made manifest (**un***folded*) through the mechanism of consciousness. When consciousness causes this to occur it becomes *explicate* and forms what Bohm calls the *explicate order* of reality.

To Bohm, the manifestation of all form is simply the result of innumerable shifts between the implicate and explicate order of reality and that there is no limit to what can be made explicate out of the implicate order (the abundant universe in which there is no shortage of anything). It's all in there, enfolded in the implicate order in the form of energy, just waiting for us to bring it forth and make it explicate.

I would add that it is our use of the tools of Radical Manifestation that enables us to focus the right kind of consciousness — Spiritual Intelligence — on what is already there in the implicate order with a view to making it explicate. Mental intelligence alone is not enough.

## Tasks:

**1.** Make a list of what you would like to draw from the implicate order — the field of infinite abundance — and manifest into existence. Give each one a time frame and indicate which of the three levels of intention it is based in, and how it might relate to the ones above it.

**2.** For each one, follow the Six Steps to Radical Manifestation:

i       Become aware of the need.
i       Clarify and give precise language to what you want to create.
iii      Visualize the end result in as much detail as possible.
iv      Feel the emotions of already having received it.
v       Hand it over completely to Spirit to do the creating for you.
vi      Drop all attachment to having it.

The important thing to realize with the above is that the first four steps are achieved with mental and emotional intelligence. The last two can only be achieved through Spiritual Intelligence and require that we treat them as spiritual practice.

As I have said many times, it is my contention that with all of this kind of work which requires us to suspend all our old beliefs about the nature of reality, we desperately need tools to help us do the spiritual work, whether it be forgiveness or manifestation. We are not well enough equipped yet to pull it off on our own.

For that reason, we have created an Online Radical Manifestation Program as a powerful tool to help you in manifesting what you want in your life. Go to *www.radicalmanifestation.com* and click on Online Radical Manifestation program on the left menu.

# Create Heaven-on-Earth

In 'Becoming Awake' Assignment #8, I suggested that you write up a purpose statement and to imagine what kind of mission you might have come in with. I also asked you to make the purpose statement bigger than you and let it pull you into it. In 1999 I was asked to do the same thing and, as you probably already know, I came up with the following statement:

*"My mission is to raise the consciousness of the planet through Radical Forgiveness and to create a world of forgiveness by 2012."*

My concept of a *world of forgiveness* was not simply that people would just get along better and forgive each other for things that occurred in the kind of world we live in now. No, what I was holding the intention to create was in line with what has been foretold in many prophecies and ancient writings, as well as spelled out in a number of contemporary books, including one of my own. The essence of it was that there would be a dramatic shift in consciousness that would create conditions on earth that would bring together the World of Divine Truth and the World of Humanity. Fear would yield to love and we would be living in harmony, Oneness and bliss. In other words we would have heaven-on-earth. It is foretold that this is likely to happen around 2012, hence this date in my mission statement.

When I wrote that mission statement I could not conceive that it was even remotely possible. I had only been teaching Radical Forgiveness for two years and even though I knew it was highly effective, I had no comprehension as to its power to change the world in any way at all, let alone create heaven-on-earth. Now I do. But I need your help. Let me explain.

I began this book with a story about Steve Parker, a soul returning from his incarnation. As you know, his Angel of Incarnation was Harley and together they reviewed Steve's journey.

In an earlier book, written in 2003, I tell the story about Harley — yes, the same one — preparing a rookie soul (Jack Barber) for his first incarnation. Being a novice, Harley has to tell him about how things work on planet Earth, what to expect, who his parents will be and so on. But the story really heats up when in the middle of the book, Harley gets the message from *on high* that Jack will have a very special and demanding mission to carry out that, if he does it right, could literally change the world. (You will probably recognize the soul of Jack since he is in the world of form right now appearing as a very public figure.)

The following, much condensed excerpt from that book, picks up the story where Jack is given his mission. I would like you to read it because it will suggest to you how you, and many thousands of others, can help me make my mission become reality without the need for the other, less attractive aspect of the prophecy story — death and destruction on a massive scale. Enjoy.

## The Mission Is Revealed

My basic schooling having come to completion, the moment had come for me to learn about my mission. I was very scared. All I had learned about how things might be in the World of Humanity had made me think twice about even taking on the ordinary human assignment, let alone doing something really special and, more than likely, extremely challenging.

"Sit down, Jack," Harley said. "I have something to tell you which quite frankly surprised me when I got it relayed to me from Higher Command."

"Is it my mission, Harley?" I pleaded. "Please tell me! I can hardly wait to know what it is."

"Your mission is to become the President of the United States, heal the soul of America, awaken the human race and bring about world peace."

"Harley, you've got to be joking. I don't even understand what that means!" I was almost hysterical by now.

"Why are you doing this to me, Harley?" I demanded. "I just wanted an ordinary incarnation. This is way over the top for me!"

"Don't panic, Jack. It's all being worked out in advance. We've got a huge team of angels working on it — all very old souls who will be able to support you every step of the way, so don't look so worried."

I was totally stunned, confused and afraid. Why me? I thought. I don't want this kind of responsibility. I am not an old, experienced soul like the ones Harley had sent down before, so why was I being picked for something so big?

"Why this and why now?" I asked.

"Well, do you recall that Universal Intelligence decided to expand its consciousness by first creating us and then experiencing through us the three dimensional world of separation?"

"Yes," I nodded.

"Well, the experiment is more or less over. Enough souls have been through the experience on Earth to have magnified the awareness of the nature of Oneness, so the expansion of consciousness has been achieved. The need to create separation through wars, strife, hunger, discrimination, torture, abuse, pain and suffering has been satisfied. We can wake people up now.

"The Awakening will start in America and will spread out from there. This has always been the soul destiny of America, Jack, and everything that it is experiencing 'now' is in preparation for the Awakening even though at this time the majority of the population is still asleep.

"America will experience a major collapse quite soon. However, we have set it up to give humans the choice to heed the warning signals about a breakdown and make the choice to awaken before it gets bad, or to resist the Awakening and go through the kind of cataclysmic event that all the predictions through the centuries have foretold. The choice is to awaken and be present in the heaven-on-earth scenario or perish in the process of re-sisting it.

"But it will be up to you to create the conditions for breakdown to begin so the warning signs are clear and unmistakable. But, don't worry, you will have help.

"I mentioned earlier that you would be partnering with another soul who would play out the necessary dramas with you to enable the mission to be accomplished. His role will be to help you heal the soul of America first so it will be a position to lead the rest of the world into its own Awakening. To do that he has agreed to mirror America's shadow material so it can be healed."

*[Harley spends a long time explaining how Eric, (soon to become Shadeem) will become this terrible dictator, use weapons of mass destruction against his own people, be ruthless in destroying any resistance to his rule, renege on agreements and treaties, go to war with another country in order to steal their oil, try to kill the President of the U.S. and so on. He also explains how this triggers the shadow of the U.S., since everything he has ever done, the U.S. has done too.]*

"So what America hates in Shadeem is simply a reflection of the contents of America's shadow. Is that it?" I asked.

"That's correct," said Harley. "And what's more, the collective conscious-ness of America, which yearns to heal and move on from its painful past, has created Shadeem precisely for this purpose. And there will be others be-sides Shadeem but they will come after.

"America has deep wounds which it hasn't been able to heal on its own. It needs someone like Shadeem and those that follow to help it heal. But in the end, Jack, it's going to take you to finally make that happen when you become President. Only then can it lead the rest of the world out of the darkness."

The importance of the words Harley had just uttered was not lost on me. I was going to have to take the lead in teaching the nation that our enemies are our teachers and are offering us a chance to heal our collective soul.

"I hear you," Harley, I said, "But even from up here that looks like a hard sell. It's pretty hard to imagine how a President like me with only half a brain, zero language skills and a twitch would be able to convince the Congress that this isn't a half-crazed notion proposed by someone who ought to be locked away in a mental institution!"

"It's not going to happen like that, Jack," said Harley, reassuringly. "You're right, though. You'll never convince anyone of this through argument and reason. No, it will come about through an energetic realignment in the overall field of consciousness shared by all who live in America.

"Besides you and Eric, there is another soul who has volunteered to play a very key role and to contribute mightily to the first phase of the physical breakdown. Like you and Eric, he has an enormously loving heart, otherwise he could not do this.

"His way of creating extreme separation will be to first create an extremely distorted division between the religions of Islam and Christianity. He will create what is known as a very fundamentalist version of Islam and will use that to stir up intense hatred against America.

"He will attract to him others who feel that America has become too imperialistic, greedy, arrogant and concerned only with furthering its own interests throughout the world, and together they will plot the destruction of America.

"While it will look like madness, it is all part of the Divine plan. It will first bring America and then the rest of the world to the brink of the breakdown so that it can ultimately choose to break through.

"What these souls do next will change everything. They will simultaneously hijack two commercial airliners. They'll dive bomb one of them directly into a nuclear power station, causing a huge explosion that could do incredible damage to the power station.

"Their intent, of course, is to cause the massive release of radioactive material in order to kill millions of Americans, but we'll intervene to make sure that doesn't happen. There'll be no need for that much death and destruction.

"The other plane will head towards the White House but again we'll intervene. That kind of mayhem is not necessary. It is the symbolism that counts. It's necessary for Americans to feel their vulnerability. Just knowing that it might easily have happened will be enough."

"So what does it take to heal the shadow of a country, Harley?" I enquired.

"What does one have to do? What will I have to do?"

"Actually, Jack, not a whole lot," replied Harley. "We have created a very simple technology for healing shadow stuff. It's called Radical Forgiveness and since it is quick, simple and easy to do, anyone can do it.

"If enough people do the Radical Forgiveness process on all the *perceived villains* to reach a critical mass sufficient to create a shift in consciousness, an Awakening will occur. There would then be no need for any further wars or anything like that. And it wouldn't take very many to create that critical mass. Less than 900,000 people would probably do the trick."

"That's incredible," I said. "After all that has happened over so much earth time, a simple technology like that can heal it?"

"Yes," said Harley. "You will stumble on this technology at the right moment, and you will use it to heal some of your own personal wounds. That's why we gave you some in your early life — so that you would experience the healing power of Radical Forgiveness. Having healed some of your wounds, you will then realize that Radical Forgiveness can be utilized to heal the country and, as a collective, become Awakened.

"You will get Congress to fund a worldwide Radical Forgiveness project that will dissolve the victim archetype once and for all and enable everyone to truly forgive themselves and others, drop all grievances and appearance of separation and move into Oneness. That will raise the vibration of humanity to a very high level.

"You will create support only for things that improve the human condition and support the environment. You would call for a re-examination of all human values and lead people towards a way of life that leads to genuine happiness and fulfillment based on the spiritual principles of giving and receiving, infinite abundance for all, mutual support, community and so on. That's the kind of leadership you will create when you awaken, Jack. You will still be President — not a politician in the old sense of the word — but a true leader in the very fullest sense of that word.

"By the end of your term you will have changed the world, Jack. You will have set humanity on a new course. You will have raised the consciousness of the planet and well before 2012, created a world of forgiveness, love and harmony out of chaos, fear and despondency. Good luck, Jack!"

# Postscript

The first edition of *A Radical Incarnation,* the book from which the foregoing was excerpted, was published in April 2003. In the light of what has happened since then, anyone might be forgiven for assuming that this story was not about a fictional character called Jack Barber at all; rather that it was a thinly veiled attempt to poke fun at George W. Bush.

Though I must admit I did allow myself some latitude in this direction, (though not much of that comes through in the excerpt), that was not my real aim. My true intention for writing the book had a higher purpose than that. It involved then, and still does involve, my helping to fulfill my mission to *"raise the consciousness of the planet through Radical Forgiveness and to create a world of forgiveness by 2012."*

The parallels I make between the characters in the fantasy and the real characters playing out world events are interesting, but the truth is I was throwing you a *red herring.* It's not about George Bush at all. It's about you. Harley was describing **your** incarnation and your mission. You are Jack. We are ALL Jack.

Harley was preparing all of us for when we would see the TRUTH of what is happening in the world and become willing to transform it. The question is, how do we do it, and where do we go from here?

As you may have heard, many predictions have been made about the likelihood of 2012 being the year when real serious breakdown occurs. For example, Nostradamus foresaw cataclysmic change on a global scale at around this time, including massive earth changes and violent political upheaval. 2012 is significant in many ancient writings, such as those in the biblical Book of Revelation as well as the traditional texts of the Mayans, the Hopi Indians and other indigenous peoples. The Mayan Calendar ends December 2012. Many of Edgar Cayce's predictions for the new millennium concerned political upheaval on a global scale and *earth changes* around this time that would be cataclysmic in nature.

143

The predictions all speak of there being two phases. The first phase would involve death and destruction on a massive scale and would last for some years. The second phase they describe as being a sustained period of peace, harmony and tranquility (2,000 years), such as humans have never before experienced.

However, Gregg Braden, in his book *The Isaiah Effect* suggests that what the prophets were actually seeing were alternate realities that, through the complexities of time warps, were becoming available simultaneously. This means we have a choice. We either wake up now and choose the peaceful version of reality, or be forced to transform in the ways described in the prophecies.

However, time is running out. If as Braden suggests, the Awakening can indeed take place without our having to go through a series of cataclysmic events, and that is our choice, we must begin to align with each other NOW to make that the reality. This is the only way we can, in Harley's words, "create heaven-on-earth" by 2012.

If ever we needed a technology to help us do this, now is the time and Radical Forgiveness is it. If enough people use it and focus their energy through its use, it has the potential to change mass consciousness and, if done in sufficient numbers, bring about world peace.

The first step is to work on ourselves. By reading this book and doing the exercises, you are already doing it and raising your vibration accordingly. To create world peace Braden quotes a mathematician saying we need approximately 880,000 people all vibrating at a high rate to pull it off without the need for a cataclysmic event. Your contribution will therefore be invaluable.

I have always said that world peace is a spiritual issue — not a political one. When we, as a group of people spread around the globe holding the same vibration, use the Radical Forgiveness technology to create PEACE, we will be more powerful than any government, politician, corporate entity, church or world leader.

**Task:**
To do work at this level Go to *www.radicalforgiveness.com* and select *World Peace Project* under the *Radical World Peace Strategy.* This will take you to a part of the site devoted to providing you with a number of online Radical Forgiveness instruments that you can use AT NO CHARGE. One of the instruments is a forgiveness worksheet on Saddam Hussein. There is also one on Osama bin Laden.

We live in a holographic universe. That means that even the smallest part of it, when separated from the main hologram, still contains the whole. That means that you are the soul of America. Everything that America has been or is now, you are — shadow as well. That's why it is possible for you to heal America just by engaging in these simple, consciousness raising activities.

Your involvement will demand very little of your time. The instruments are simple and designed to instantly create a coherent pattern of Radical Forgiveness that resonates with the part of the Unified Field that is in you and in every American person. The effort required is minimal.

Now, what about the Awakening? The story made it seem that, in order to make the Awakening happen, it would take someone with the power of the President of the United States to do it. We know now that is not the truth. As I have said before, the real message of the story is that we are ALL Jack, and it is up to us to awaken to the truth of who we are.

The Radical Forgiveness technology is a consciousness raising technology in and of itself, and it will create the Awakening. For the first time ever, it seems, individuals now have an opportunity to change the world. If we focus our efforts together, it will become a matter of certainty.

145

9/11 was a huge wake up call orchestrated by Spirit to help all of humanity see what we have created and to give us the opportunity to choose again. Two thousand years ago, the effect of our *not getting it* was not immediately catastrophic — though it has of course proven to be so over time. (It has actually brought us to this place and situation. If we had heeded Jesus's teachings, we might well have had heaven-on-earth before now.)

If we fail this time, however, the effects are likely to be immediate, global in scope and catastrophic in nature. This could be our last chance to get it right, and the stakes could not be higher.

Until now it has been almost impossible to physically bring huge numbers of people together in common cause. Imagine trying to get in excess of 880,000 people together in one place to do something. Now, with the Internet at our disposal, it has become very easy.

By coming to our web site and making a commitment to heal yourself first and the world second, you will be contributing energy to the greatest project ever undertaken — to awaken Humanity from its dream and to create heaven-on-earth.

### Are You Ready to Help Create 'Heaven-on-Earth?'

**Task:**
Go to www.radicalforgiveness.com and select *Strategy #10, Radical World Peace* from the left menu. Follow the instructions.

# Listen to Your Body

It is fitting, I believe, to end this section on growth assignments by entreating you to listen to your body. That's because your body has great wisdom and it is giving you messages all the time that, if heeded, will always point you in the right direction and will be of assistance to you with virtually all of the other assignments in this section. It will tell you who you still need to forgive for example, where you are still holding grief, and so on. It will also help you establish your purpose, because deep down it knows everything.

Before going any further we ought to clarify that when we talk about the body in this way, we are acknowledging the fact that mind, body and spirit are one and that when we talk about the body having wisdom we are invoking the whole body/mind/spirit continuum. That includes each of the three forms of intelligence that we posses — mental intelligence, emotional intelligence and Spiritual Intelligence. The physical body is both the antennae for wisdom that comes in from Spirit in the form of subtle energy and the instrument for communicating that wisdom to ourselves and others.

If there is one thing that has proven the body's wisdom and its inherent ability to give us answers to yes/no or true/false questions, it is kinesiology, or muscle testing. Health practitioners have been using it for years as a tool to get information from patients about, for example, the suitability of a medicine or a food, or whether something is good or bad for a patient and so on. Basically the idea is that you ask a person to raise their arm to shoulder level and to tense their deltoid muscle in resistance to a downward pressure that you exert on their arm. You then make a statement that is either true or false. The muscle will go weak if the answer is false and the arm will drop down under your pressure, while if it is true it will remain strong. By doing this repeatedly, you can get answers to very sophisticated and complex questions.

But the person who has elevated it to scientifically validated method of calibrating qualities of consciousness is David Hawkins, M.D., Ph.D. best selling author of *Power versus Force*. He has created a very sophisticated form of muscle testing using triple blind verification to test the accuracy of the method. This is the gold standard for measuring the efficacy of medical procedures, so it is seen as solid proof that it works.

Another method that is easier and equally as reliable is to use a pendulum. You first find out which way a pendulum will consistently move when the answer is yes, and which it way it will move when the answer is no. There is nothing mystical about this and anything will do as a pendulum. All it is doing is amplifying the subtle messages that are coming from your body which otherwise might be hard to detect.

The body is always communicating with us in very direct ways, telling us where energy is stuck, where we are holding anger, fear, responsibility, grief, sadness and so on. If you pay attention to your body it will tell you a great deal about your life and what you need to do to in any one moment that will be to your highest good.

Some of the messages coming from the body are easy to read and we shall enumerate some of them in a moment. But before going there, let's go back to first principles for a moment and consider what is happening at the spiritual level around *body*.

It is interesting to note that *body hatred* is almost universal. How many people do you know who love their bodies just the way they are? Even though we blame it on the media for creating unrealistic stereotypes, I am certain that it goes a lot deeper than that. In fact, I suspect that it has a lot to do with our purpose for being here which, as I am sure you are tired of hearing, is to experience separation. But not just as an idea. It has to be experienced emotionally. Since *an emotion is a thought attached to a feeling,* you need a body to provide the feelings. Why else would a spiritual being, who is free to move around at will within the World of Divine Truth decide to lower its vibration and become encumbered with a body that is dense, heavy, and prone to regularly breaking down?

If the body is our spiritual vehicle for taking us into and through the deep pain of separation as a profoundly emotional experience, is it any wonder that we are not only obsessed with our bodies, but essentially hate them for precisely that reason? Even though our memories of existence prior to incarnation are for the most part non-existent, isn't it possible that a part of us might remember what it is like to be just Spirit and not encumbered with a body?

And might we not have some resentment about having to carry this burden? If so, doesn't it make sense that we might project all our guilt and rage about being separate and in pain onto our body? After all, having taken on a body as a symbol of separation, it follows that the body must also symbolize the intense pain that inevitably accompanies the sense of separation.

As we awaken to the truth that the experience of separation is what we came into this life to have, and that this body of ours is serving us in every way possible, perhaps we can develop a more loving relationship with it, no matter what it looks like or how often it breaks down. We can begin to take back all that we have projected onto it out of our hatred of it and develop a deep sense of gratitude for all that it does for us. Love and appreciation for our body is a natural outcome of the Awakening experience.

That said, now let's look at how we might become aware of and interpret the messages that the body is continually sending out to us. The primary method by which our bodies communicate is through pain and discomfort. This is our early warning system.

Like any early warning system, if it remains unheeded things are likely to escalate. If we ignore the messages that the body is giving us, disease and breakdown is likely to occur.

What you do with this medically is up to you and your medical advisor, but from the point of view of how this messaging might assist you in your Awakening process and guide your psycho-spiritual growth there are some general guidelines that can be useful.

The following are just a few of the observations that the vast majority of practitioners who have studied the mind/body/spirit continuum and those who have studied the science of psychoneurimmunology agree upon as being reasonable assumptions.

**Task:**
Check whether or not the following have any application to you:

☐ Pain or discomfort on the right side of the body might indicate that you have issues relating to the masculine energy, while discomfort that is located on the left side might suggest issues relating to the feminine energies.

| ☐ Applicable ☐ Marginal ☐Not Applicable |
| --- |

☐ Discomfort in the head and neck area — headaches, watery eyes and neck pain can indicate an inability to make decisions.

| ☐ Applicable ☐ Marginal ☐Not Applicable |
| --- |

☐ Tension in the shoulders is associated with accepting and holding too much responsibility — carrying the weight of the world on your shoulders.

| ☐ Applicable ☐ Marginal ☐Not Applicable |
| --- |

☐ Discomfort in the stomach area — indigestion, acid reflux, etc., might indicate your resistance to accepting something. "I just can't stomach it any more." "I can't digest it." "It makes me sick to my stomach that . ."

| ☐ Applicable ☐ Marginal ☐Not Applicable |
| --- |

☐ Guilt, particularly repressed sexual guilt, is often the cause of problems in the lower abdomen and groin area and invariably the cause of people carrying excessive and disproportionate weight in that area of the body.

☐ Applicable ☐ Marginal ☐Not Applicable

☐ Problems with hands and arms might indicate a tendency to overreach or underreach in how life is approached.

☐ Applicable ☐ Marginal ☐Not Applicable

☐ Resistance to moving forward and wanting to run from something can be inferred from having problems with your legs from the knee down and the feet. You may be feeling trapped or stuck where you are.

☐ Applicable ☐ Marginal ☐Not Applicable

Caroline Myss in her book *The Anatomy of Spirit* revealed in a very carefully researched way which psychological and emotional issues end up being held energetically in certain areas of the body linked to the chakras system. [Chakras are energy centers that exist not in the physical body but in the etheric body and yet they are linked energetically to particular organs of the body.]

## The Chakras

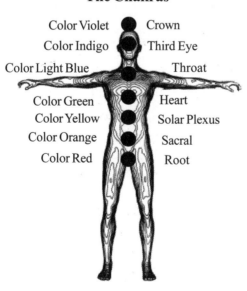

Color Violet — Crown
Color Indigo — Third Eye
Color Light Blue — Throat
Color Green — Heart
Color Yellow — Solar Plexus
Color Orange — Sacral
Color Red — Root

**Task:**
Examine the following information drawn from Myss's work on the kind of psychological issues held in each of the chakras. If you have any symptomology in the areas of the body indicated by Myss as being associated with a particular chakra, look to see what or who might be activating those issues in you. This will clue you in on what might need to change in your life, who to forgive and so on.

CROWN: *(Skin, bones and muscle)*
**Issues:** Values, ethics and courage. Humanitarian concerns. Ability to see the big picture. Faith and inspiration.

| Symptoms | Resonant Issue | Persons Implicated |
|----------|----------------|--------------------|
|          |                |                    |

THIRD EYE: *(Brain, nose, nerves, eyes, ears, nose, pineal, pituitary)*
**Issues:** Truth, intuition, self-awareness, learning ability, emotional intelligence.

| Symptoms | Resonant Issue | Persons Implicated |
|----------|----------------|--------------------|
|          |                |                    |

THROAT: *(Thyroid, neck, mouth, parathyroid, hypothalamus)*
**Issues:** Personal expression, communication, strength of will, following one's dream, using one's power to create. Addiction, judgment, decision making ability.

| Symptoms | Resonant Issue | Persons Implicated |
|----------|----------------|--------------------|
|          |                |                    |

HEART: *(All chest area and thymus gland)*
**Issues:** Love, hatred, resentment, bitterness, grief, anger, hope self-centeredness, loneliness,commitment, forgiveness, compassion, hope, trust.

| Symptoms | Resonant Issue | Persons Implicated |
|---|---|---|
| | | |

SOLAR PLEXUS: *(Stomach, liver, gall bladder, pancreas, adrenals, mid-spine)*
**Issues:** Fear, intimidation, trust, personal power, confidence, honor, care of self and others. Co-dependency and sensitivity to criticism.

| Symptoms | Resonant Issue | Persons Implicated |
|---|---|---|
| | | |

SACRAL: *(Genitals, pelvis, low back, appendix, hips, bladder)*
**Issues:** Sex, money, creativity, blame, guilt, control, integrity and honor in relationships.

| Symptoms | Resonant Issue | Persons Implicated |
|---|---|---|
| | | |

ROOT: *(Body support, coccyx, rectum, feet, immune system, prostate)*
**Issues:** Basic security, feeling at home, ability to stand up for self, social and family law and order, tribe.

| Symptoms | Resonant Issue | Persons Implicated |
|---|---|---|
| | | |

**Note:** You will notice that some issues will involve several chakras and will cross reference each other, especially where emotions are concerned. For example anger will show up in the root chakra towards someone who has made them feel insecure or not worthy to be on the planet. It will show up in the sacral over such issues as sexuality, control or restriction of creativity. And so on through all the chakras. Similarly with other emotions.

It will take some detective work on your part to sort out what the symptomology might mean from a psychological and emotional standpoint, in particular what core negative belief is underneath that symptom. For example, psychotherapist Lawrence LeShan who worked with cancer patients all his life discovered that all cancer patients had the same core-negative belief. *"If I show up as who I am, no one will love me. Therefore, in order to be loved, I have to be someone I am not."*

But as you continue to awaken and begin to listen more attentively to your body and hear what it is saying, the more you will understand. And, in all probability, the more healthy you will become. That's because once the message has been heard and acted upon — through forgiveness, acceptance, compassionate response, release, etc., the energy stuck in that particular chakra and associated body parts will dissipate. In all likelihood the symptoms and the pain will disappear also.

Finally, I would like to share one particular observation of my own for which I have no scientific proof but continues to be borne out in every workshop that I do in which there is a person attending who is either challenged with or has had what is known as Chronic Fatigue Syndrome.

I have yet to meet one person with that condition who was not brought up in a home which demanded of them total perfection. Usually it was the mother who was the perfectionist but whether it was father or mother, or both, the message received was the same: *no matter how hard I try to please them, it will never be enough.*

154

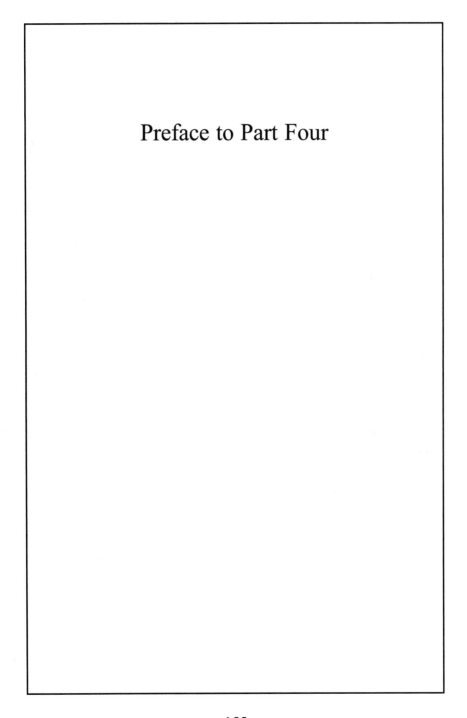

# Preface to Part Four

# A Bridging Technology

In many places in the foregoing pages I have made reference to the tools of Radical Forgiveness and have suggested very strongly that you make use of them. Why? you might ask.

The answer is that Radical Forgiveness is grounded in a paradigm that is, as yet, difficult for us to fully grasp, so we need these tools to help us bridge the *consciousness gap* between the old paradigm (victim consciousness) and the new paradigm (Divine order).

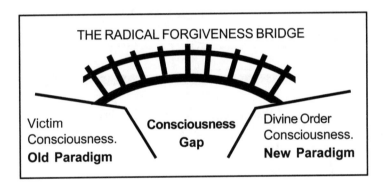

THE RADICAL FORGIVENESS BRIDGE

Victim Consciousness.
**Old Paradigm**

**Consciousness Gap**

Divine Order Consciousness.
**New Paradigm**

What gets us over that bridge is not our mental intelligence, nor even our emotional intelligence. Rather it is our Spiritual Intelligence that bridges the consciousness gap and connects us with the Divine Plan. The question then arises: what activates our Spiritual Intelligence? The answer is our use of the tools. Without using the tools it would (given our current level of consciousness), be almost impossible to bridge the gap. Trying to do it mentally will not work.

A good way to explain where we are now in our consciousness insofar as how we tend to see the world now — our cosmology according to the old paradigm, if you will — is to use the tapestry analogy.

## The Tapestry Analogy

When we look at the back of a tapestry, we see only untidiness, chaos, random colors, random movement, knots, mistakes covered over, and very little meaning. It might even look quite ugly.

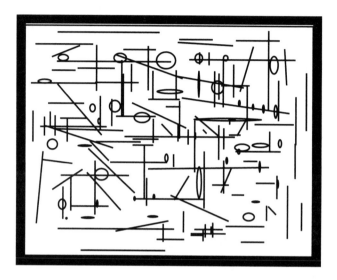

Looked at from the old paradigm point of view, this is how we see life — as a sequence of seemingly random events; very untidy; a lot of loose ends; a matter of good or bad luck; virtually meaningless; nothing connected in any coherent way.

But, if we were to turn the tapestry over we would see on the other side a beautiful picture. Then we would know that everything on the back had meaning, including every knot, every thread, every seemingly meaningless event. Our own lives are like that tapestry. At this time we can see only one side and it seems to be the reality. But the reality is actually on the other side, though we are not yet privy to it.

Fortunately we only have to be willing to be open to the idea that there is a reality beyond our current consciousness and that there is perfection in everything. The tools provide the means to express that willingness.

The tools are as follows: (See Part 4 and the Appendix for details.)

The Radical Forgiveness Worksheet
The Three Letters
The 4 Steps to Radical Forgiveness Process
The Release Letter
The Free Online Radical Forgiveness Worksheet Program
The 13 Steps to Radical Forgiveness CD
The 13 Step Radical Self-Forgiveness/Self Acceptance CD
The 7 Step Process for Radical Forgiveness CD
The Multimedia Radical Empowerment Program
The 'Satori' Radical Forgiveness Game

Though in this book I have only given you the first four since the others are all on different media or online, all the tools embody the assumptions of Radical Forgiveness. These are:

**1. We live in at least two worlds at the same time, and the soul bridges the two and is fully aware of both.**

**a) The World of Spirit:** A spiritual reality — essentially mysterious and beyond our five senses to perceive it and beyond our mental capacity to comprehend it.

**b) The World of Humanity:** The objective reality that we see *out there* with our five senses. It is the setting in which we live our every-day lives as spiritual beings having a human experience i.e. *a feeling experience.*

For the vast majority of the time, our personality self is only aware of the World of Humanity — the world we know and experience through our five senses and extensions thereof such as microscopes and other instruments. It is the setting in which we live our everyday lives. It is a world of physical form, duality, separation, time and space, change and uncertainty.

159

The World of Spirit is the world of spiritual reality and inner experience. Essentially, it exists as a world without form, changeless, and without time, space or separation (i.e. the other side of the tapestry).

These two worlds are not geographically distinct. They are not places at all, of course, just different frequencies. This accounts for how we exist in both worlds at the same time. It is simply a matter of adjusting our receiver (our body/mind) in such a way as to receive a wider range of frequencies. This is what we mean by expanding our awareness.

Making the journey from the World of Spirit to the World of Humanity (incarnating), in order to experience the qualities inherent in the World of Humanity as a means of spiritual growth, is a choice that our soul makes. However, in order that the experience be genuine the soul must develop amnesia about the World of Spirit during the incarnation.

**2. Life is not just a random set of events without purpose or intelligence.** What appears to be haphazard is really the unfoldment of a Divine plan that is totally purposeful in terms of our spiritual growth.

**3. We are co-creators with Spirit in the circumstances of our lives,** and we get precisely what we want (there being no exceptions). The extent to which we resist (judge) what we get, determines whether we experience it as either joyful or painful.

**4.** Whenever we get upset with another person (or organization), **they are resonating in us something that we have condemned in ourselves and denied, repressed and projected onto that person or thing.**

**5. We incarnate with a *mission*** — an agreement with Spirit that we would do certain things to meet a karmic debt, complete a soul level contract, assist in transforming energies within the human condition, or simply to have experiences.

**6. Our soul will always move us in the direction of healing** and will keep on creating situations that offer us the opportunity to see the *error* in our thinking or unconscious beliefs. People come into our lives to lovingly *act out* the parts over and over until we heal the error. Herein lies the gift.

**7. The people we dislike the most are our greatest teachers,** for they may be offering us the opportunity to heal by either:

(a) mirroring what we hate in ourselves and have denied, repressed and projected onto them,
(b) forcing us to look at something we have repressed and which remains as a core belief or unhealed trauma,
(c) keeping us on track with our mission.

**8. What appears to be happening in the objective world is merely illusion** — it is just a projection of our consciousness (our unconscious beliefs, ideas, attitudes, etc.) To know what these are, look what is showing up in your life. Life is simply a mirror.

Each time we use the tools we are reminded of these principles and in time begin to embody them. Likewise, each time we use one of them it is akin to going over the Radical Forgiveness bridge and hanging out energetically — if only for a while — in the new paradigm.

Every one of the tools — and workshops too for that matter — takes us through five distinct stages in the actual experience of Radical Forgiveness. These are as follows:

## 1. TELLING THE STORY
Having your story *heard, witnessed* and *validated*, is the first step to letting it go. Likewise, the first step in releasing victimhood is to own it fully. So, in this step, someone (perhaps yourself if you are doing it alone) willingly and compassionately listens to you tell your story without judgment, accepting it totally as your truth in the moment.

161

## 2. FEELING THE FEELINGS

Your feelings represent your authentic power. Your strength lies in your vulnerability and your willingness to show up as fully human. You cannot heal what you don't feel. When you access your pain, this is the beginning of your healing.

## 3. COLLAPSING THE STORY

This takes the power out of the victim story you made up. It's mostly interpretation, anyway. The tools help you retrieve the energy you had invested in your story and helps you to move towards the truth.

## 4. REFRAMING THE STORY

Here we replace the *illusionary* story with another story - the Radical Forgiveness *story*. This one says that what appeared to have happened, far from being a tragedy, was in fact exactly what you wanted to experience and was in that sense, absolutely perfect.

## 5. INTEGRATING THE NEW STORY

It is necessary to integrate that change at the cellular level. That means integrating it into the physical, mental, emotional and spiritual bodies so it becomes a part of who you are. Breathwork, walking, physical work, doing worksheets, etc.

This process is easily seen and is in fact made explicit in the Radical Forgiveness worksheet, the instructions for which are given in the pages that follow. In the worksheet the integration is done in two ways. First by writing your responses, and second, by reading everything out loud from the beginning of the worksheet to the end. Using your voice is a very powerful way to integrate a shift into your body which, by the way, is where your stories live.

In order to completely understand these notes and instructions, I would suggest you download a worksheet immediately from the website, assuming you haven't already done so, and use the instructions to help you fill one out when you are ready. (www.radicalforgiveness.com)

# PART FOUR

## The Tools of Radical Forgiveness

# The Radical Forgiveness Worksheet
## (With Additional Instructions)

### 1. Telling the Victim Story

[Questions to ask yourself: What am I upset about? With whom? Why? What did he/she/it/they do to me? Really BE the victim. No spiritual overlays or making excuses. Attach your pre-written story to this but add anything you want to on this page to increase your victimhood.]

### 2a. Confronting the Person Who Victimized You
"_____ ,I am upset with you because . . . "

[If the event occurred when you were a child or your victimizer had power over you in some other way, it is probable that you were not able to shout back, retaliate or confront the person. So this is your chance to do so. Tell the person (or organization) how much it has hurt or damaged you. Really BE the victim. No spiritual overlays or excuses. Tell it like it was or is.]

### 2b. Feeling the Feelings
Because of what you did (are doing), I FEEL:
[Identify your real emotions here. Use feeling words. Sad, angry, betrayed, hurt, rejected, resentful, rageful, vengeful, etc.]

### *(Now Acknowledging Your Own Humanness)*

**3.** I lovingly recognize and accept my feelings, and judge them no more. I am entitled to my feelings.

| Accept: | Willing: | Skeptical: | Unwilling: |
|---|---|---|---|
| | | | |

**4.** I own my feelings. No one can make me feel anything. My feelings are a reflection of how I see the situation.

| Accept: | Willing: | Skeptical: | Unwilling: |
|---|---|---|---|
| | | | |

[This is an empowering step because you are taking your power back by owning responsibility for your feelings. When we say others *make* us feel angry, we give them power over us.]

[Secondly, your feelings give you a tremendous amount of feedback about how you perceive the situation — usually as a victim. Knowing that, you are then in a position to choose to see it differently and then alter your feelings about it.]

## 5. Holding Judgments and Expectations

My discomfort was my signal that I was withholding love from myself and
_____ by judging, holding expectations, wanting _____ to
change and seeing _____ as less than perfect. *(List the judgments,
expectations and behaviors that indicate that you were wanting him/her/them to
change.)*

[When we judge a person (or ourselves) and make them wrong, we with-
hold love. Even when we make them right, we are withholding love, because we make our love conditional upon their *rightness* continuing. Any
attempt to change someone involves a withdrawal of love, because wanting them to change implies that they are wrong (need to change) in some
way. Furthermore, we may even do harm in encouraging them to change,
for though we may act with the best intentions, we may interfere with their
spiritual lesson, mission, and advancement.

For instance, if we send unsolicited healing energy to someone because
they are sick, we are in effect making a judgment that they are not OK as
they are and should not be sick. Who are we to make that decision?
Being sick may be the very experience they need to have for their spiritual
growth. Naturally if they request a healing, then it becomes a different
matter entirely, and you do all you can in response to their request. Nevertheless, you still see them as perfect.

It is also revealing to see how many of these judgments and expectations
you are making about yourself. Remember — ***if you spot it, you got it!]***

## *(Now Beginning to Collapse the Story)*

**6.** I now realize that in order to feel the experience more deeply, my soul has
encouraged me to create a BIGGER story out of the event or situation than it
actually seemed to warrant, considering just the facts. This purpose having been
served, I can now release the energy surrounding my story by separating the facts
from the interpretations I have made up about it.

[Much of our pain is in our being invested, not so much in the **facts** of what
happened, but in what we ***made up*** about what happened. e.g. Granddad died
— *he abandoned me.* My mother divorced my Dad — *she drove my father
away from me.* My husband cheated on me — *I must no longer be sexually
attractive.* I was sexually abused — *all men will hurt me.* My father was emotionally unavailable to me — *I'll never be enough.* So here you would list the
main interpretations and indicate whether the level of emotion and attachment
you have around each interpretation is still, at this moment in time, high, medium, low or at zero.]

166

### 7. Core-Negative Beliefs I Either Made Up From My Story or Which Drove the Story. *(Check Those That Apply)*

☐ I will never be enough. ☐ It is not safe to be me. ☐ I am always last or left out. ☐ People always abandon me. ☐ It is not safe to speak out. ☐ I should have been a boy/girl. ☐ No matter how hard I try, it's never enough. ☐ Life's not fair. ☐ It is not good to be powerful/successful/rich/outgoing. ☐ I am unworthy. ☐ I don't deserve. ☐ I must obey or suffer. ☐ Others are more important than me. ☐ I am alone. ☐ No one will love me. ☐ I am unlovable. ☐ No one is there for me. ☐ Other_____

## *(Now Opening to a Reframe)*

**8.** I now realize that my soul encouraged me to form these beliefs in order to magnify my sense of separ-

| Accept: | Willing: | Skeptical: | Unwilling: |
|---|---|---|---|
|  |  |  |  |

ation so I could feel it more deeply for my spiritual growth. As I now begin to remember the truth of who I am, I give myself permission to let them go, and I now send love and gratitude to myself and _____ for creating this growth experience.

## *(Noticing a Pattern and Seeing the Perfection In It)*

**9.** I recognize that my Spiritual Intelligence has created stories in the past that are similar in circumstance and feeling to this one in order to magnify the emotional experience of separation that my soul wanted. I am recognizing some clues in my life that provide evidence that, even though I don't know why or how, my soul has created this particular situa-tion, too, in order that I learn and grow.

| Accept: | Willing: | Skeptical: | Unwilling: |
|---|---|---|---|
|  |  |  |  |

[Here you would list similar stories and feeling experiences (as in 2b) and note the common elements in them. The kind of evidence to look out for might be as follows:

**i. Repeating Patterns.** This is the most obvious one. Marrying the same kind of person over and over again is an example. Picking life partners who are just like your mother or father is another. Having the same kind of event happening over and over is a clear signal. People doing the same kind of things to you, like letting you down or never listening to you, is another clue that you have an issue to heal in that area.

**ii. Number Patterns.** Not only do we do things repetitively, but often do so in ways that have a numerical significance. We may lose our job every two years, fail in relationships every nine years, always create relationships in threes, get sick at the same age as our parents, find the same number turning up in everything we do, and so on. It is very helpful to construct a time-line like the one like Steve did (see Page 46), except

167

that you might fill in all the dates and note all intervals of time between certain events. You might well find a meaningful timewise correlation in what is happening.

**iii. Body Clues.** Your body is giving you clues all the time. Are you always having problems on one side of your body or in areas that correlate to particular chakras and the issues contained therein, for example? Books by Caroline Myss, Louise Hay and many others will help you find meaning in what is happening to your body and what the healing message is. In our work with cancer patients, for example, the cancer always turned out to be a loving invitation to change or to be willing to feel and heal repressed emotional pain.

**iv. Coincidences and Oddities.** This is a rich field for clues. Anytime anything strikes you as odd or out of character, not quite as you'd expect or way beyond chance probability, you know you are onto something.

Where once we thought things happened by chance and were just coincidences, we are now willing to think that it is Spirit making things happen synchronistically for our highest good. It is these synchronicities that lie embedded in our stories, and once we see them as such, we become free then to feel the truth in the statement that "my soul has created this situation in order that I learn and grow."

## *(Noticing the Projection and Taking It Back)*

**10.** I now realize that I get upset only when someone resonates in me those parts of me I have disowned, denied, repressed and then projected onto them. I see now the truth in the adage, "If You Spot It, You Got It!" It's me in the mirror!

| Accept: | Willing: | Skeptical: | Unwilling: |
|---------|----------|------------|------------|
|         |          |            |            |

**11.** (X)_____ is reflecting what I need to love and accept in myself. Thank you _____ for this gift. I am now willing to take back the projection and own it as a part of my shadow. I love and accept this part of me.

| Accept: | Willing: | Skeptical: | Unwilling: |
|---------|----------|------------|------------|
|         |          |            |            |

**12.** Even though I may not understand it all, I now realize that you and I have both been receiving exactly what we each had subconsciously chosen and were doing a dance with and for each other to bring us to a state of awakened consciousness.

| Accept: | Willing: | Skeptical: | Unwilling: |
|---------|----------|------------|------------|
|         |          |            |            |

**13.** I now realize that nothing you, _____,
have done is either right or wrong. I am able now to
release the need to blame you or anyone else. I release the need to be right about this, and I am **WILL-
ING** to see the perfection in the situation just the way it
is.

| Accept: | Willing: | Skeptical: | Unwilling: |
|---|---|---|---|
|  |  |  |  |

**14.** I am willing to see that, for whatever reason, my
mission or *soul contract* included having experiences
like this and that you and I may have agreed to do this
dance with and for each other in this lifetime. If it is for
the highest good for both of us, I now release you and
myself from that contract.

| Accept: | Willing: | Skeptical: | Unwilling: |
|---|---|---|---|
|  |  |  |  |

**15.** I release from my consciousness all feelings of *(as in Box # 2b):*

## *(Now the Reframe Statement)*

**16.** The story in Box #1 was your Victim Story, based in the old paradigm of reality
(victim consciousness). Now attempt a different perception of the same event (a
reframe), from your new empowered position, based on the insights you have
experienced as you have proceeded through this worksheet.

*(It may simply be a general statement indicating that you just know everything is
perfect, or a statement that includes things specific to your situation if, that is, you
can actually see what the perfection is. Often you cannot. Be careful not to do a
reframe that is based in World of Humanity terms. Note any positive shift in feeling
tone.)*

I now realize that . . .

[The reframe is the thing that people have the most trouble with. They often try
to give some explanation of it in World of Humanity terms; what they learned
from it about their life, or a decision they made, etc. Those are not invalid
interpretations of course, and they might come into the category of *gifts*. But
they do not indicate a grasp of the spiritual perfection that was the underlying
purpose of the situation — which is the reframe we are looking for.

The original situation as in Box #1, the victim story, was framed by all the
thoughts, preconceptions and beliefs that you had about it, and for the most
part, they are those that naturally arise out of victim consciousness.

The reframe therefore is an invitation to change the experience by changing
your perception of it — in other words, changing how you frame it. Instead of
referencing it from the victim standpoint, you frame it with the idea that there is
Divine perfection in the situation even though you cannot yet see it.

169

This is often very difficult to accept, but the good thing about it is that it does not require that we see WHY it is perfect, or that we must GET the lesson involved. It is nearly always beyond our ability to comprehend anyway, so it's a waste of time trying to figure it all out.

You are, in effect, *trying on* the new paradigm; of feeling out what it might feel like to adopt the idea of spiritual perfection. In that sense then, Radical Forgiveness is a *fake it till you make it* process.

Even so, it is possible that, as a result of doing the reframe you might begin to see the situation in a completely different light and begin to move into a feeling of gratitude for the person. If not immediately then perhaps at some future time.]

## *(Now the Final Proclamations)*

**17.** I completely forgive myself, _____and accept myself as a loving, generous and creative being. I release all need to hold onto emotions and ideas of lack and limitation connected to the past. I withdraw my energy from the past and release all barriers against the love and abundance that I know I have in this moment. I create my life and I am empowered to be myself again, to unconditionally love and support myself, just the way I am, in all my power and magnificence.

**18.** I now SURRENDER to the Higher Power I think of as _____and trust in the knowledge that this situation will continue to unfold perfectly and in accordance with Divine guidance and spiritual law. I acknowledge my Oneness and feel myself totally reconnected with my Source. I am restored to my true nature, which is LOVE, and I now restore love to _____ . I close my eyes in order to feel the LOVE that flows in my life and to feel the joy that comes when the love is felt and expressed.

**19.** A Note of Appreciation and Gratitude to you _____ . Having done this worksheet I now . . . .

. . . I completely forgive you, _____ , for I now realize that you did nothing wrong and everything is in Divine order. I bless you for being willing to play a part in my Awakening — thank you — and honor myself for being willing to play a part in your Awakening. I acknowledge and accept you just the way you are.

**20.** A Note to Myself . . .

I recognize that I am a spiritual being having a spiritual experience in a human body, and I love and support myself in every aspect of my humanness.

# Writing Three Letters

This functions in a similar fashion to the Radical Forgiveness Worksheet but is spread out over a longer period. It involves writing three separate letters, ideally one per day, to the person, persons or organization you feel have wronged or hurt you in some way. While it certainly works wonderfully when you are really upset about something that has just happened, it will work just as well on something that may have happened a long time ago — even if the person is dead or nowhere around.

This is because, like all forgiveness processes, you never tell the person you are in fact forgiving him or her, or that you have forgiven. They do not need to know and you should have no need to tell them. If you do feel that need, then look at your need to control or manipulate the other person (because that's what telling them that you have forgiven them would amount to). They will know anyway, energetically, that something has changed between you. None of the three letters that you write in this process should ever be sent.

## Letter #1

This letter represents Stage #1, Telling the Story, and Stage #2, Feeling the Feelings. The idea is you write an accusatory letter to your victimizer telling him or her how you have been damaged, wounded, hurt and so on. Remember, you always start from where you are and that means feeling victimized. You make no excuses for the person and show no mercy whatsoever. All you know is that you are the victim in this situation. Vent all your anger and rage in this letter. Hold nothing back. You can threaten vengeance of the vilest kind if it makes you feel good. Keep writing until you have nothing left to say. Get everything out. It might take many pages.

The process of writing this letter may cause you to shed a lot of tears — tears of rage, sadness, resentment, and hurt. Let them flow. Have a box of tissues beside you. If you are angry, scream into a pillow or do some physical activity to help you feel your anger. ***Remember, under no circumstances mail this letter!***

## Letter #2

This is best done the next day, after you have cooled down somewhat and slept on it. It is good to allow a dream cycle to occur between each letter so each one can be processed by the subconscious mind.

This second letter represents Stage #3 in that it helps to begin the process of collapsing the victim story and retrieving the energy invested in it. It is where we begin to realize that while the pain is in what actually happened, the suffering is in what we have made up as our story. There is often a huge difference.

This letter therefore should begin to help you sort out what is true versus what you imagined was true or that which was your interpretation. In that sense, a part of this letter might become something of a dialogue with yourself about what happened as if you were musing about the whole thing trying to make some sense of it. This in itself will help begin to collapse the energy field around the situation or event.

Towards your victimizer, you might begin to sound a little more conciliatory. Your writing might carry a little less anger and vengeance, although you still do not let the person with whom you are angry off the hook for what you believe he or she has done to you.

Nevertheless, it is in this letter that you begin to cut the person some slack and begin to imagine what might have made the person do this to you. You make some effort to walk in their shoes for a while in order to develop some understanding of what made them do it. For example, people who have themselves been wounded are likely to act out their repressed rage on someone else. People who abuse children are nearly always people who were themselves abused as children. People who were abandoned as children are likely to abandon others later in life.

In this letter you should make an effort to bring some compassion, understanding, and generosity, as well as the possibility of some sort of forgiveness, into the equation. However, since the belief is still intact that you have been victimized by this person, it can only be forgiveness of the traditional kind — definitely not Radical Forgiveness.

## Letter #3

The third letter, written at least one day after the second, represents Stage #4, the Reframe. In this one, you attempt to describe a new interpretation of the situation based on the principles of Radical Forgiveness. In other words, you write that you now realize that the person was, at the soul level, acting out of love by doing what they did because it was what you (your soul) wanted to experience. You had in fact recruited him or her to do it not TO you but FOR you. It is even likely that you and the other person had agreed up front, prior to incarnation that he/she provide this experience for you — a soul contract in other words. All you are now able to feel towards this person is gratitude.

(Remember, Radical Forgiveness is always a *fake it till you make it* proposition. This letter will almost certainly come into that category. You write it as if you believed it totally, with as much fervor and skill as you did with the previous two letters. Your body needs to get it!)

Nevertheless, the likelihood is that you will feel a whole lot better for doing these three letters and, if the situation is still ongoing, it will probably resolve itself fairly quickly thereafter.

**Note:** We have designed a whole weekend workshop around the Three Letters process. It has proven extremely helpful to people over the years and is offered regularly. It is called simply, The Radical Forgiveness Workshop. (See Appendix, Page 195.)

# The 4-Step
# Radical Forgiveness Process

Unlike most of the other tools which you only use in moments of quiet reflection some time after an upset, this is the process to use right there in the moment when something upsetting happens. Going through these four steps in your mind will stop you going to Victimland and becoming stuck there for a long time.

It is a good idea to have the four steps printed on the back of a business card to keep in your purse or wallet. Better still, commit it to memory.

**Step One.** *"Look what I created."*
This is where we get to take responsibility for having created the situation — for whatever reason. The principle is that we are creating our life moment by moment and that each occurrence is designed and created as a learning experience. God does not make mistakes.

**Step Two.** *"I notice my judgments and love myself anyway."*
When bad things happen we curse the situation and automatically fall into judgment about it, looking for someone to blame. It's all part of being human and we have to love ourselves for doing it. It's all part of the learning process. This connects us with what actually is happening in our body and mind and brings us into the present through our feelings. Our energy then shifts quickly and allows us to go to the third and fourth steps of this process.

**Step Three.** *"I'm willing to see the perfection in the situation."*
This invites us to be willing to entertain the possibility that the situation is nothing more than the Divine plan unfolding. This is the Radical Forgiveness step. Another way to say it is "I am willing to see the hand of God in the situation."

**Step Four.** *"I choose the power of peace."*

A profound sense of peace arises when we express the willingness to see the perfection in the situation. By accepting Divine purpose is served in this situation we choose to use the power of peace in whatever actions are required of us. The power of peace is found when we are totally present in the moment, acting with clarity and focus to do whatever may be required and totally aware of our feelings.

**The 4-Steps Worksheet**

On the next three pages you will find an actual worksheet based on the four steps process. This simply provides an opportunity to externalize the process. The third step is expanded to include some thoughts about how the perfection is revealing itself.

*This worksheet can be downloaded as a 2-page letter-sized sheet from www.radicalforgiveness.com. Click on downloads.*

# 4 Steps To Radical Forgiveness Worksheet

## Step One:  *"Look what I created."*

This first step reminds us that we are the creators of our lives and that we have in fact set up all the circumstances in the situation we find ourselves upset about, to help us learn and grow spiritually - or heal a wound or core belief that keeps us out of our joy and bliss.

☐ AGREE       ☐ WILLING       ☐ OPEN       ☐ SKEPTICAL       ☐ UNWILLING

## Step Two:  *"I notice my judgments and love myself anyway."*

This step acknowledges that, as humans, we automatically attach judgments, interpretations, questions, and beliefs to situations. We quickly create a victim story and try to lay blame on others. It's part of being human. So we must recognize and lovingly accept our feelings. They give us good feedback about our consciousness - and they clue us in to our subconscious wounds and core-negative beliefs.

☐ AGREE       ☐ WILLING       ☐ OPEN       ☐ SKEPTICAL       ☐ UNWILLING

**I Am Feeling:** *Angry, sad, frustration, vengeful, etc.* _____

**My Wounds:** *Betrayal, abandonment, abuse, hurt, rejection, stolen from, let down, lied to, cheated on*  _____

## Step Three:  *"I am willing to see Divine Order in this situation."*

    **a)** This is where we attempt to reframe the story by becoming willing to be open to the idea that, in the sense that our Higher Selves have created this situation (as we said in Step One), then our life is unfolding exactly as it needs to unfold and everything is in Divine order. It is what we want and need for our soul's journey. Nothing wrong is happening and there is nothing to forgive. *(The key word here is WILLINGNESS. Only a very small amount of willingness to be open to this possibility is required.)*

177

**b)** This step also asks that we entertain the possibility that we have attracted the people with whom we are upset specifically to provide us with this experience. They are doing these things to us because our soul and theirs have contracted to do it for each other. They are not therefore our enemies but are our *healing angels* because without them, we would not have the opportunity to grow or to heal those core-negative beliefs.

☐ AGREE    ☐ WILLING    ☐ OPEN    ☐ SKEPTICAL    ☐ UNWILLING

**Core Beliefs:** *(Circle the ones you identify with?) Not good enough; Have to be perfect to be loved; Unlovable; Don't deserve love; Not worthy to receive; Ugly; Always will be abandoned; Always will be betrayed;*

**c)** This step also offers you the opportunity to see that what you see and hate in other people is precisely what you cannot stand in yourself and have denied, repressed and projected on to them.

*The things I dislike about* _____ *, are:* _____

_____

**Sorry about this but, *IF YOU SPOT IT, YOU GOT IT!***

*"I am willing to recognize that* _____ *is mirroring something about me that I have denied and repressed, and I am now willing to love and accept that part of me, whatever it is, right now in this moment and to thank* _____ *for giving me the opportunity to heal."*

☐ AGREE    ☐ WILLING    ☐ OPEN    ☐ SKEPTICAL    ☐ UNWILLING

## Step Four: *"I choose the power of peace."*
By accepting that Divine purpose is served in this situation and that what appears to be occurring may be illusionary, we choose to surrender to Spirit and to feel peace, knowing that we can use the power of peace in whatever actions are required of us.

*"I release all the feelings, judgments and resentments I had in Step One and Choose Peace."*

☐ AGREE     ☐ WILLING     ☐ OPEN     ☐ SKEPTICAL     ☐ UNWILLING

Note to _____ : *Having done this worksheet I now feel........*

Note to Myself: *Having done this worksheet I .....*

**Miracle Journal:** Note any miracles that occur over the next few days as a result of doing this worksheet.

© 2003 Colin Tipping,

# The Release Letter

Date: _____     Name _____

I, _____ , hereby grant you, my Higher Self, my Soul, my Super-Conscious Mind, my DNA, my cellular memory, and all parts of myself that might want to hold onto unforgiveness for whatever reason, permission to release all of the misunderstandings, unfounded beliefs, misinterpretations, and misguided emotions, wherever they may reside, whether in my body, my unconscious mind, my DNA, my conscious mind, my subconscious mind, my unconscious mind, my chakras and even my Soul, and I ask all those who want the best for me to assist in this releasing process.

I, _____ , thank you, my Soul, for creating the experiences that created the unforgiveness and I realize that on some level they have all been my teachers and have offered opportunities for me to learn and to grow. I accept the experiences without judgment and do hereby release them to the nothingness from which they came.

I, _____ , do hereby forgive _____ .
I release him/her to his/her highest good and set him/her free. I bless him/her for having been willing to be my teacher. I sever all unhealthy attachments to this person and send him/her unconditional love and support.

I, _____ , do hereby forgive myself, accept myself just the way I am, and love myself unconditionally just the way I am, in all my power and magnificence.

I, _____ , do hereby release myself to my highest good and claim for myself freedom, fulfillment of my dreams, wishes and goals, clarity, love, full expression, creativity, health and prosperity.

Signed: _____     Date: _____

181

# Tools On CD, DVD and Online

### 1. Online Worksheet — Radical Forgiveness

For more than six years we have offered this online interactive version of the Radical Forgiveness Worksheet and, at the time of writing, it has been used over 17,000 times. People have just loved it. It is based on a worksheet which is not quite the same as the one in this book, but it is similar enough that you will be able to use it with ease. Most people find it to be as powerful, if not more so, than the paper version. It has Help screens, informational pop-ups and you can print out the final worksheet. Go to www.radicalforgiveness.com and click on Online Programs.

### 2. CD — The 13 Steps to Radical Forgiveness

This CD is actually sold separately as a companion CD to the book, *Radical Forgiveness, Making Room for the Miracle* and actually included in the pack containing the book on CD. It is also included as one of the CDs in the *Radical Forgiveness Power Pack.* (See Appendix)

The 13 Steps to Radical Forgiveness is the audio equivalent of a Radical Forgiveness worksheet. It needs to be heard rather than read which is why I am not including the text in this book or anywhere else for that matter. It is important that you listen to it and respond verbally.

As you would expect, it takes you through the same five stages as all the other tools. I start out by asking you to bring to mind your *story.* Then I encourage you to feel your feelings about what happened. (Is this beginning to sound familiar to you now? — it should.) Then I ask a further 11 questions that require an actual verbal response from you. The response to the question is Yes in every case, even if you would rather say No. (You should know why by now.)

The process only takes about 8 minutes but it is very potent. It's amazing what results from doing this simple process. It is not hypnotic, nor even meditative, so you can do it with your eyes open. You can even listen to it in the car so long as you remain attentive to the road.

The CD also features five songs, one by Debi Lee and the others by Karen Taylor-Good. These songs just happen to be our favorites! (See Appendix - Page 200)

### 3. CD — 13 Steps to Radical Self-Forgiveness/Self-Acceptance

Obviously, the process itself is similar to the other 13 Steps process, except that the questions are different. A lot of people find it much more difficult to forgive themselves than to forgive others, so this is real blessing for them. This one has a song by Karen Taylor-Good that you will love called, "I Forgive You — Me." She wrote it specially for this CD and for our weekend workshop on Self-Forgiveness.

### 4. CD — The 7 Step Process to Radical Forgiveness

Until recently, this process was reserved for use by the Radical Forgiveness Coaches when in session with their clients. We felt at the time that it needed to be done in the presence of a Coach.

However, it has turned out to be such a powerful process that we wanted to make it available to more people. So we have put it on one of the CDs in the *Radical Forgiveness Power Pack.* (See Appendix, Page 198.) It does however need to be treated with respect and done according to the parameters that I feel are necessary, such as a safe space where there will be no interruptions, a time set aside specifically for the process which takes about 20 minutes and the presence of someone nearby to hold the space safe for you.

It is to be listened to and is an *eyes closed* process. Verbal responses to certain questions and statements are required and there is two minutes of breathwork involved — that being Stage #5, the Integration phase.

## 5. Multimedia Pack — The Radical Empowerment Program

The objective I had for creating this program was that I felt people who had been exposed to the Radical Forgiveness concept wanted something that would help them make Radical Forgiveness a permanent way of responding to the challenges and irritations that inevitably come along in the course of daily living. In other words to have Radical Forgiveness so firmly anchored in their being that it would become a habit — a default response to life. (See Appendix, Page 189.)

I called it Radical Empowerment because it put together the technologies of Radical Forgiveness and Radical Manifestation; Radical Forgiveness to heal the past and retrieve energy invested in the past, and Radical Manifestation to use that same freed up energy to create the future. *(Radical Forgiveness + Radical Manifestation = Radical Empowerment.)*

The pack contains 9 hours of video by me on 5 DVDs plus 5 CDs, packaged with workbooks, worksheets and a Journal in which you record the events that have occurred that day and what tool you used to dissolve the energy around it and so on. There is one page in the Journal for every day for a period of 12 months. Radical Forgiveness should be a way of life by the time the 12 months are up while, by then, the Radical Manifestation process should be in full swing, helping you create the life you want.

## 6. Game — 'Satori' The Radical Forgiveness Game

This incredible board game is like a mini workshop. It literally plays you. It's a great way to share Radical Forgiveness with friends and family because it is easy to play, requires no prior knowledge but yet provides people with wonderful insights and healing opportunities. (See Appendix, Page 198.)

*(For further details of these and other programs and products, see the Appendix and the web site, www.radicalforgiveness.com.)*

# APPENDIX

# Radical Manifestation —
*The Fine Art of Creating the Life You Want*

***Using Spiritual Intelligence to
Manifest Money, Weight Loss,
Happiness and More.***

Colin Tipping gave us the spiritual technology of *Radical Forgiveness* to help
heal our past and raise our vibration. He
also gave us tools that help us deal with
life on an everyday basis.

In this book, he now provides, in his
own unique way, a powerful technology
with which to create the future.

Lately, there has been an upsurge of interest in, and an increasing
awareness of, the possibility that life is not just something that happens to us, but that we actually have a hand in creating it through our
consciousness. Underlying all of these approaches is the idea that if
we understand and use the Law of Attraction, we can create the reality we want.

Tipping explores how we might begin to align with this idea and begin
creating consciously, using not mental programming techniques primarily, but the power of our own innate Spiritual Intelligence. It is
this that marks Tipping's approach out as different from many others.

This book is sold as a stand-alone item on its own account, available
in bookstores and from our own web site, but it is also a constituent
part of the multimedia learning program entitled, ***"Colin Tipping's
Radical Empowerment Program,"*** featured on page 189.

# Colin Tipping's
# **Radical Empowerment Program**

***The Program That Helps You to Stay Awake AND
Create Your Future!***

**How the Program Works** — It gives you the tools that activate the power within you to create virtually anything you desire. It teaches you how to use your ***Spiritual Intelligence*** to raise your vibration, create your reality and accelerate your spiritual growth.

**A Powerful Technology** —The combination of *Radical Forgiveness* (to heal the past) and *Radical Manifestation* (to create the future), is a very simple technology, but the effects are dramatic. The struggle is over. You simply take the information provided and put it into practice, using the Spiritual Intelligence Training Processes to ***supercharge the results.***

### *A 12-Month Program*
We recommend that for optimum effect, you commit to working this program for 12 months. By the end of that period, your vibration should be significantly higher and your ability to manifest your reality much enhanced.

# Colin Tipping's
# Radical Weight Loss Program

This is no ordinary weight loss program. It makes no mention of diets, exercise routines or drastic changes in lifestyle. **Wow! Isn't that refreshing?** So what's the trick?

Over the years we noticed that when people who were overweight did our Miracles workshop they automatically lost pounds soon after. All indications were that they had been carrying excessive weight as a form of protection against a perceived attack or as a way of holding guilt, grief, anger and other emotions. The forgiveness work had enabled them to let it go. Hence this unique approach to weight loss.

So, the only things you are asked to *give up* in this program are the stories that were responsible for your putting on weight in the first place. And we provide you with all the tools with which to do it.

*For details go to www.theradicalweightloss.com*

# Colin Tipping's
# **Radical Money Program**

Whether you are a millionaire aspiring to become a billionaire, or you're flat broke and want to get back on your feet financially, this program is for you.

Among the many things included is a special software program entitled *"Prosperity Through Spending."* Don't worry, it's not as crazy as it sounds. The money you spend is *virtual* money.

The principle is that your *income set-point* is directly related to your *spending set-point.* Since the purpose of this program is to raise your income set-point so as to create a fourfold increase in your real income over two years, one of the ways to do it is to have you get used to spending ever increasing amounts of *virtual* money. So it's fun as well as effective. Also included are a book, audio CDs, a workbook, pen and calculator all nicely contained in a leather portfolio.

*For details, go to www.radicalmoneyprogram.com*

191

# *A Radical Incarnation (Yours!)*

*In this "spiritual fantasy", Colin reveals the soul contract made between George W. Bush and Saddam Hussein — **and you** — to create Heaven on Earth.*

With this book, Tipping has once again demonstrated his gift for making spiritual principles simple and applicable to everyday life. He has done it by bringing that ability to bear on the largest issue of the day — **world peace.**

The way he does it is that you, the reader, get to accompany the soul of Jack Barber as he is carefully tutored and prepared by Harley, his senior Angel of Incarnation, for his upcoming human experience on planet Earth, along with another soul with whom he will interact on the world stage to bring the world to a point of breakdown and then break*through*. Could it be . . . ?

Is it possible that these two souls made a soul agreement to do this? Is George Bush actually Jack Barber? Is Saddam a *"healing angel"* for America, mirroring its shadow? Are we playing a part too? *You bet we are!*

It will have occurred to you by now that the power you have to create your own reality includes the possibility of creating a wholly different world. You can literally create world peace. And it only takes a few of us to actually form the critical mass necessary to make it happen.

But we can't look to this, or any other president, to awaken and lead humanity to do the same. We must do it. It is not Jack Barber's or even George Bush's *radical incarnation.* It's yours. It's ours. ***World peace is our choice.***

As with his other books, Colin provides the on-line technology with which to transform ourselves and — hopefully without the need for breakdown — to heal America, raise the consciousness of the planet and create Heaven on Earth.

A somewhat abridged version of this book is now on CD for those who prefer to listen.

It is entitled *Soul Contract.* (Colin has added Tony Blair as one of the key players.)

## Help Create World Peace

Go to *www.radicalforgiveness.com* and click on the **America's Healing Project** link on the Home page. You will get an invitation to participate in the process of creating world peace by:

1. Forgiving America's enemies, including Saddam, Osama bin Laden and others
2. Forgiving America, UK and its leaders
3. Forgiving yourself and your personal enemies
4. Making a Radical Apology to blacks, Native Americans, Jews, Arabs, etc.
5. Accepting a Radical Apology, if due
6. Empowering a vision of world peace

***The Secret to the Creation of World Peace
is Radical Forgiveness!***

# Spirituality in Business is HOT — *This <u>Book</u> is Hot!*

A <u>MUST-READ</u> for anyone interested in being at the forefront of the new business cultural revolution characterized as *'social capitalism.'*

It shows how a cutting edge, employee development system that uses a spiritual viewpoint, the **Quantum Energy Management System,**\* can transform the culture of any organization in ways that benefit everyone involved — while boosting the bottom line.

<u>**An audio CD is included as a sample of the technology.**</u> *(Hard cover version only.)*

In this ground-breaking book, Colin Tipping shows how any organization can be transformed with this enterprise-wide, personal development program that:

> • *reduces* incidents of conflict, discord, dissent, sabotage, cynicism, racial tension, etc.

> • *increases* morale, job satisfaction, loyalty, cooperation, team spirit and overall productivity.

**A Radical Approach to Increasing Productivity, Raising Morale and Preventing Conflict in the Workplace.**

\*For information about **The Quantum Energy Management System** go to www.QEMSystem.com

# Workshops and Training Programs

## 1. Workshops

We regularly offer a variety of ways of experiencing Radical Forgiveness in a group setting, so take a look at our web site, *www.radicalforgiveness.com* for descriptions of the workshops and check the calendar for dates.

We draw your attention to these two workshops in particular since they are ideal for people who have read the book that started it all — *Radical Forgiveness, Making Room for the Miracle (also on CDs)* — and/or the one you are holding in your hands, and wish to go deeper into the Radical Forgiveness experience.

### A. The Miracles Workshop

This workshop is for those who wish to have some personal assistance and guidance from Colin in moving through some deeply rooted forgiveness issues in a safe and loving space with no more than 15 people participating. This incredible workshop will free you from the tyranny of the past, open the space for miracles to occur, completely alter your world view, and change your life for the better in so many different ways. A truly transformational experience!

### B. The Radical Forgiveness Workshop

This workshop is a more classroom based learning experience but includes practical experience with many tools of Radical Forgiveness but primarily the Three Letters combined with Art Therapy work.

195

## 2. Online Programs

A FREE, interactive *Radical Forgiveness* process is available on our web site for anyone to use at any time.

We also offer three on-line programs for SELF-EMPOWERMENT. These are self-guided and can be done at your own pace. Great for releasing self-blame, guilt and shame and for enhancing one's self-esteem.

   a) Radical Self-Forgiveness Program
   b) Radical Self-Acceptance Program
   c) Releasing Toxic Secrets Program
See *www.onlinehealingprograms.com*

## 3. Certification Training Programs

If you like to teach, run book study groups and discussion groups, coach others and to be of service to people, or you are already in the healing arts, coaching, pastoral counseling or mental health professions, you might wish to examine our training programs. They offer certification as:

a) A Recognized Book Study Leader

b) A Recognized Radical Empowerment Discussion Group Leader

c) A Certified Radical Forgiveness Therapy Practitioner/Coach *(This is for already qualified professionals.)*

A certified RF coach is able to provide professional coaching sessions with people or small groups, either in person, over the phone, or on-line. This training is offered as a home-study program.

*For details, go to www.radicalforgiveness.com*

# 'Satori'

## *The Radical Forgiveness Game*

The *Radical Forgiveness* experience can be had in many different ways. This board game is one of them and it's fun as well as transformational.

As you would expect, it takes you through the same five stages of *Radical Forgiveness,* but this time in the context of a game that can be played by up to five people and takes between 1-1/2 and 2-1/2 hours to play.

It is a lot of fun, and in the playing of it, energy is moved in the same mysterious way as it does in all the other forms of the *Radical Forgiveness* experience. It is not necessary for all players to have prior knowledge of *Radical Forgiveness.*

Players pick a 'story' card to play with *(which invariably resonates a real situation for them)*, and they all start in Victimland. They proceed around the board which spirals in towards the center, the objective being to reach the full Satori, which is, as you know, the Awakening.

We find ourselves picking up Beliefs and Energy Blocks along the way, finding ways to release them, or project them onto someone else. There are three Gateways to get through — the Gateway to Awareness; the Gateway to Shift Happens and the Gateway to Surrender.

# DVD/CD Packages

## 1. The Radical Forgiveness "Power Pack"

The 3 DVDs and 2 CDs in this pack are specially designed to empower you to make Radical Forgiveness work for you in your everyday life. The DVDs give you approximately five hours of high quality video recording of Colin speaking to you about Radical Forgiveness, the tools it provides and the metaphysical under-pinning of the approach. We are confident that you will find the content fascinating, empowering, completely down-to-earth and practical.

## 2. Radical *Self*-Forgiveness & *Self*-Acceptance DVD/CD Set

This pack includes a 90 minute DVD by Colin which gives all the reasons why his radical approach to forgiveness works for self-forgiveness and self-acceptance and reveals the secrets of how to release guilt, self-recrimination, shame and self-criticism in an easy 10 step process.

The pack also includes a CD which has the 13 Steps to Radical Self-Forgiveness and Self-Acceptance on it. It also features a song by Karen Taylor-Good, specially written for this CD, and guaranteed to bring you to a place of self-love, entitled *"I Forgive You — Me."*

# Colin Tipping's Radical Relationships DVD/CD Set

This is not your ordinary *Cosmo-type* program designed to help you improve your love life. Rather, the aim is to discover the TRUE purpose of all relationships and learn how to apply it to our lives. The true purpose can be described as follows:

*Without exception, no matter whether it be a long term committed relationship or a momentary interaction with the person at the supermarket checkout counter, ALL relationships offer opportunities to learn, heal and grow spiritually. We each become for each other, by soul agreement, magnets for growing.*

Understanding how we create such opportunities and enroll others in our healing dramas is the key to finding the true value in any relationship. On the DVDs we explore the spiritual dynamics of relationships and how they are grounded in the Radical Forgiveness philosophy. To help us find the functionality in any relationship we need tools that help us connect, through our Spiritual Intelligence, to the (unknowable) Divine plan. On one of the CDs there are two well proven tools that help us do just that. Expect miracles!

**DVD #1:** Introduction to Radical Forgiveness
**DVD #2:** Radical Relationships
**CD #1:** Jill's Story
**CD #2:** a) 13 Steps to Radical Relationships
        b) The 7 Step Radical Forgiveness Process

*For details, go to www.radicalrelationship.com*

# The 13 Steps

## To Radical Forgiveness CD

Sometimes the written word simply isn't enough. There are some things that just have to be heard. *The 13 Step Process is one of those.* Just reading it would have very little effect, so rather than put it in the book Colin has chosen to make it available to you in its most potent form — as a recording.

There is an introduction, of course, and then Colin asks 13 questions to which you simply answer "Yes." That's it! It's so simple you can't imagine that it could change anything, but it does.

There are also four songs featuring our very own **Karen Taylor-Good.** Her work is so wonderful and so in alignment with Radical Forgiveness, it's like she is part of every workshop we do — if not in person then on CDs. You will simply love these four songs. If you want more — come to our website for a selection of her other CDs.

At **$13.00** + S & H, it is the most valuable recording you will ever own. It will almost certainly improve your relationships — and perhaps even save your life! Don't delay — order today!

### *Lots More to Buy on the Website too!*

### *www.radicalforgiveness.com*